Tokoroa

£2

17/12

Also in this series

Emerging Pluralism—The Samoan
Community in New Zealand, by David Pitt
and Cluny Macpherson

Tokoroa
Creating a community
D L Chapple

Longman Paul

Longman Paul Limited
182–190 Wairau Road,
Auckland 10, New Zealand

Associated companies, branches and
representatives throughout the world

© Longman Paul Limited 1976
First published 1976

ISBN 0 582 71744 2 (Cased)
       0 582 71745 0 (Paper)

Cover photograph by permission of
the South Waikato News

Filmset in Hong Kong by
T.P. Graphic Arts Services
Printed in Hong Kong by
Dai Nippon Printing Co (HK) Ltd

Contents

List of Maps & Illustrations

Additional photographs may be found between pages 146 and 153

Editor's Foreword

There has been a quiet revolution in New Zealand since the war. In the wake of urbanization and industrialization new communties have emerged both in the suburbs of the old cities and in the countryside. The social sciences in New Zealand have not given the new communities enough attention, leaving their discovery to the national mass-media who often see only the sensational and the extraordinary. Not only are many of the new towns such as Tokoroa growing more rapidly than any other part of New Zealand but, more significantly, new and different social forms are developing in them. The generalizations so common in the New Zealand social science literature, based on vague statistical abstractions, meaningless imported models, or myths about a single New Zealand social structure, need to be radically re-examined.

In this perceptive book Don Chapple gives us an insight into one of the new situations in New Zealand. It is a situation which has its own logic and dynamic, a situation which makes Tokoroa very different from Auckland, Wellington, or older established provincial centres. Here the class and cultural lines have not hardened as they have in the big cities. Tokoroa is a vibrant community, mobile, and active in all social and economic activites. Its citizens are deeply involved and concerned about the future of their community. In some ways perhaps, Tokoroa reflects the kinds of values and aspirations of the vanished frontier New Zealand of the egalitarian myth. The necessity and difficulty of making a living in a new industry, the isolation, and the indifference of the institutions of the outside world have created some kind of unity of purpose, some kind of identity.

Tokoroa is a new situation and new sociological methods are needed to study it. Don Chapple uses an exciting new approach to come to grips with his subject. He is most concerned with the small groups and situations of everyday life and with the common sense

vii

perspectives of the people themselves. The result is a picture of the Tokoroa behind the statistics and the surveys, a Tokoroa away from the problems projected by the television camera.

Finally, Don Chapple's book indicates how the social scientist can be helpful in the everyday world. The study of Tokoroa began in 1969 when a small group of individuals approached me to ask if the University of Waikato would help to provide information on Tokoroa's attitude to itself and its development. The sociologists duly did their survey and wrote their report and since then have remained involved. Tokoroa was however no Vicos, the sociologist only provided, and only wished to provide, information. His role in the power structure was minimal and his recommendations were never embodied in any five year plan. Don Chapple's book is in some ways a qualitative complement to the earlier quantitative studies. It is another interpretation of Tokoroa, another angle, more ideas to be chewed over by those in Tokoroa and in the world outside.

Some may say that the sociologist who simply supplies information or interpretation is not really involved in the action. A deeper involvement in action however implies hints of an undesirable influence. It is up to the people of Tokoroa to shape their own community and its future. Levi-Strauss once said it is only our own society which we can transform without destroying.

May we thank the people of Tokoroa for all their help and wish them continued success and prosperity.

David Pitt

Foreword & Acknowledgements

For readers who are expecting an orderly social survey of an industrial town, an account well supported with statistical tables and analyses of these, this book may be disappointing. I refer those readers to just such a report on the same town (see Pitt and Swain 1970). Although I have used some of the material from this main survey report, and some from the companion report on youth opinion (Pitt 1970), there seemed to be little point, and no challenge, in merely reworking these reports into book form. Rather, in compiling this study I have preferred to work after the manner of a 'bricoleur', using any kind of material at hand, and any kind which seemed to serve both my purpose of the moment and my conception of the whole. Thus, for example, Chapter 5 draws fairly heavily upon the survey of youth opinion, Chapter 6 is compiled almost entirely from neighbourhood studies written by residents themselves, and Chapter 7 leans heavily upon local newspaper reports of political affairs. Within most chapters of the book I have attempted also to vary the manner of presentation. A 'bricolage' of theoretical perspectives, survey data, biographical fragments, newspaper items, and photographs would seem to promote more active and sustained interest in the reader. At least this was my intention although I am aware that the result is not nearly as imaginative as I would like it to have been.

Because the present study aims at exploring processes rather than presenting statistical facts at a point in time, it might have been far more successful had I lived and worked in the town. Regrettably it was not expedient to do so although I visited the town many times during 1970 and 1971.

Finally it is my pleasure to acknowledge help and encouragement from a number of persons: Professor David Pitt, the editor of this series; Phoebe Meikle and Rosemary Stagg of Longman Paul; David Pitt, David Swain, Cluny Macpherson, and Edward

ix

Douglas whose various studies and survey reports I have drawn
upon; Father Ray Selby and Mr Brian Burmester, editor manager
of the South Waikato News, whose hospitality and help in
Tokoroa have been invaluable; the residents of Tokoroa who
attended the community study workshop in May 1970, and whose
discussion and writing has helped to shape this book (I have
assumed that they would wish to remain anonymous); the many
social science students of the University of Waikato who have
contributed to our understanding of the town through participation in surveys of various kinds; the several ex-residents who
contributed excellent neighbourhood studies. Mr Frank Bailey
of the University of Waikato, who did initial draughting work; Mr
Gordon Campbell of Havelock North; and N.Z. Forest Products
Limited who supplied information and graphic material.

Some very special acknowledgements must be made: to Mr
Brian Burmester who kindly offered to supply photographs; and
to Ms Margaret Oaten of our sociology department who not only
typed the manuscript but did the job with unforgettably good
humour; and Mrs Reapi Blyde for typing additional material.

D.L. Chapple

Introduction

This is being written, as I suspect most introductions are, as a postscript to the main text. Certain additions and modifications have been made to the text and there remains the task of justifying the result, and of alerting the reader to some prejudices and predilections of the author, and to peculiarities in the work itself.

What is the purpose of this study of a timber town? If I were tempted to say that the aim was merely descriptive, even a careless reader would soon uncover the deception. Description abounds, but so does evidence of selection and differential emphasis in the use of descriptive data. The criteria of selection and emphasis are influenced, inevitably, by the author's own set of values and his social ideology. Having accepted the task of producing a social study of Tokoroa, I found myself drawn more towards certain aspects of the scene than to others, and, drawn more sympathetically to some categories and classes of persons than to others. After a brief historical review (Chapter 1) in which wider presses and processes are described, the reader will find a recurring tendency toward the particular, and especially the biographical particular. With admittedly sparse material I have nevertheless indulged an interest in the drama—and often the small drama—of social life. Without this interest and this indulgence the book would never have been written. So, if a 'purpose' developed in the course of writing this study, it is that of inviting readers to observe and reflect upon some of this drama of everyday life in a new and rapidly expanding industrial community.

'Models'—those plausible patterns of meaning which we all use to help us find our way amongst complex phenomena—appear in most chapters, sometimes quite explicitly (as near the beginning of Chapters 3 and 5 and throughout the final chapter) but in other places less obtrusively. A reader with a little knowledge of sociology and cognate disciplines will detect that these explanatory models owe more to an unsophisticated social

xi

psychology than they do to any 'science' of social structures. Structural considerations have not been entirely neglected (for example, see the discussions of differential access to economic and political power in Chapters 2, 3, 5, 7, and 8). But, my interests draw me rather more towards that dynamic relationship between the person and his face-to-face reference groups than between these groups and their co-ordination into a complex whole we call 'society'. At best, I have been able only to approach the concept of community (a more personalized concept than 'society', see Burch 1969).

It will be appreciated by now that I cannot talk about 'the model' used in this study of Tokoroa. There are several models according to the particular subject area and the perspectives which are chosen. A crude structural model in which categories of people are identified and described in terms of their differential power and public status is one which recurs in the study. But the variety of model to which I tend to revert most frequently is one which may be called a 'cultural world' model. This, the social-psychological perspective mentioned earlier, grows out of case study material. It is person or small-group centred. It tries to help the observer, and reader, to understand social facts and processes *from the point of view of the actor or actors involved*. Problems of establishing and maintaining self respect and status, of 'controlling' one's social environment and enhancing one's place in it, are central to this perspective. (And the perspective itself would seem complementary to the structural one.) It is developed most fully in Chapter 3, but underlines much of the 'pluralist' discussion in Chapter 5 and the case material of Chapter 6. The perspective is again picked up and reiterated in the final chapter.

I have preferred not to be more explicit on the formulation and use of models in this study. In social studies there is, and should never be, orthodoxy—neat, standardized conceptual frames into which we squeeze our data. Model formulation is, or ought to be, an eclectic business and model use as flexible as it needs to be. We learn most about models by seeing them applied (or mis-applied) and, above all, by applying (and misapplying) them ourselves. When a student can read a sociological study and re-work the data in his mind by using somewhat different conceptual frames to those employed by the author, he is beginning to feel his strength. And if he can approach relatively raw data—in print and in real life—and shape this material into configurations of plausible and satisfying meaning which can stand the test of further inquiry, then he is entering into his full inheritance, so to speak, as a student of social life.

I have not wished to preface the various collections of raw documentary material (notably news items) with any more comment than that already supplied. To leave nothing for the reader to piece together is not to credit him with much intelligence or imagination. I can remember reading Dos Passos' *U.S.A.* with intense interest and pleasure precisely because the author invites the reader to work at fitting his vignettes together into meaningful wholes. There seems every good reason why this principle should be applied more often in sociological texts.

Chapter order, too, might present difficulties for some readers. After Chapter 2, almost any sequence could be followed so I suggest that readers 'read for interest'—and recreate whatever pattern might be inherent in the whole range of data (an exercise which I have attempted in the final chapter).

There must be weaknesses and omissions in a study such as this. On the role of organized religion in Tokoroa, I re-examined the original text and found it wanting. The result has been a compromise; I have incorporated more data in Chapters 3 and 4 and trust that churchmen and students of sociology will be satisfied. The data is still too thin—but so, too, is the material on an equally important cultural activity in Tokoroa, namely, drinking at the pub. I never mentioned, in the text, that 46 per cent of the sample of individuals in the University Survey, say that they go to the hotel 'regularly'. Compare that figure with those on church attendance (page 70 below).

The subject of communication—between all sectional interest groups, including those based upon age—is one which merits greater attention. Professor Pitt, in his preface to the University Survey (Pitt and Swain 1970) emphasizes the need for an all-round improvement in the range and quality of communication if the town is to keep abreast of its problems, especially those concerning ethnic minorities, youth, and local body affairs. For each of these areas (in Chapters 3, 5, and 7 respectively) I have said something about the quality of communication. Special aspects of communication are discussed in Chapter 8 ('Community Service and Community Action'). Chapter 6, on neighbourhood and neighbouring, provides much case material on the subject. And in Chapter 9, the problem is again raised and examined briefly with the help of a 'cultural world' model. But I will have to acknowledge that this is still not satisfactory. Raw data in these areas is not accessible to me as I write this (in Fiji) and, the publisher's deadline is too close for me to rectify the problem.

There is also a need for more material on social stratification. Data on educational attainment and incomes has been available from the 1969 University Survey, but without a whole array of supporting material the inclusion of this would not have been particularly helpful in revealing patterns of 'class'. In several other contexts, however (including this introduction), I do discuss aspects of social stratification and hope that the overall lack is not too serious. I would rather leave more explicit statement on the social structural implications of my study—including comparisons with community structures generally in New Zealand —to scholars who are better equipped to draw these out. In the following sketchy discussion I draw together and reiterate some of the scattered themes which already appear in the text.

The cystallization of social class—according to the major criteria of educational achievement, occupation, and income—is almost certainly an emerging fact in Tokoroa. Although the finer social correlates of this process I cannot verify, the fact is most evident at the extremes in location and styles of residence (see pages 52–3, 141) and is almost certainly delineated also (at least at the extremes) in the pattern of preference in voluntary association. A 'man of means' is more likely to have a larger, better appointed house in a more 'desirable' part of town. He is likely to be a member of a civic service club and to drink at the Tokoroa Club or at a private bar in the Timberlands Hotel and so on. A man with little occupational status (even though he might be earning a handsome wage) is likely to be living in a modest company house, is not likely to be a member of a civic service club and will drink his beer in the public bar of the Timberlands or the Tokoroa Hotel, and maybe at the Pulp and Paper Workers' Club. The ethnic correlates are also evident, at least at the extremes.

However, with generally high incomes (some wage earners earning more than salaried workers) and a preponderance of relatively uniform company housing available to both wage

earners and salaried workers, there remains a very broad middle
category of townsman and breadwinner who can yet escape being
'typed' on any but a ridiculously elaborate class scale. Perhaps,
in the magnitude, ethnic diversity, and social and vocational
versatility of this broad category of persons (and their families),
we have an exaggerated example of what we New Zealanders like
to think obtains in all our newer urban communities and which
probably does prevail, in good measure, in most. No 'aristocracy'
entrenched in local commerce and the professions linked by
marriage to a landed 'aristocracy' of the region. (Tokoroa is still
too new for that.) No 'old boys network' operating via exclusive
clubs to link the influential in professional and commercial
life and local political affairs. In Tokoroa, there is some evidence
to suggest the operation of a young 'old boys network' (or networks) and that the size of the town helps facilitate its efficiency.
No equation of either of the foregoing with a religious elite—
usually Anglican but sometimes Presbyterian or Catholic.
(Tokoroa has probably escaped this one, permanently.)

It would be rash to claim that Tokoroa dissolves its would-be
elites—in a round at the pub, in the common interest club, in the
local political forum, or at the interdenominational altar—just as
quickly as they are formed. Rather, we can suggest that their
public behaviour, the correlate of their greater economic and
political power, stands in less crude contrast to the majority who
wield little such power. Some of the reasons for this are nation-
wide—a stiff tax on high incomes with a redistribution for social
services, including an attractive public school system which
spreads opportunities and tends to level speech and manners.
Other plausible reasons relate to certain areas of industrial
activity. Thus, the timber, pulp and paper industry runs a hungry
labour market and has generated an increasingly confident and
powerful trade union organization. Wage earners in the industry
can eat, dress, and play more after the manner of their salaried
'superiors'. Finally, apart from the main industrial organization,
commercial and professional enterprise in Tokoroa is still relatively small-scale. Business and professional people are 'well-to-
do' rather than wealthy in the current stage of development of the
town. Increases in population and in the scale of economic activities are likely to change the picture in the direction of more con-
spicuous wealth, while a tightening of the labour market and a

weakening of union bargaining power, would be likely to throw up even sharper contrasts at the opposite end of the class scale. Tokoroa's 'egalitarianism' could eventually become indistinguishable from that which prevails (as part-fact, part-myth) in any young, small New Zealand city.

The Regional and   1
Historical Setting

'. . . the ease in working the pumice lands, and the excellent manner in which trees of many kinds grow, mark out these lands as the most suitable of any in the Dominion for afforestation.' (N.Z. Royal Commission on Forestry, 1913: xxxii)

The great volcanic plateau region of the North Island has been New Zealand's latest major frontier for settlement and industrial expansion. Five hundred years ago much of the region must have appeared formidable to the Arawa and Tuwharetoa people who had been settled for several generations in more favoured localities nearby, notably around the shores of the lakes from Rotoma to Taupo and along the Upper Waikato River valley. Fifty years ago settlement, whether of Maori or Pakeha, was still restricted largely to these localities although in the early 1920s the stage was being set for the most dramatic ecological changes in New Zealand since the expansion of dairy farming in the late nineteenth and early twentieth centuries.

This earlier development gave an important impetus to the timber industry for the rapid expansion of dairy farming in New Zealand was accompanied by an equally rapid depletion of indigenous softwood timbers used for butter boxes, cheese crates, and for building generally. This was noted even in the first decade of this century and was one concern of the 1913 Royal Commission on Forestry which was charged with an investigation into New Zealand's forest resources and afforestation potential. The Commission travelled extensively in both islands but was nowhere more impressed with what it saw than on the pumice plateau of the central North Island. Experimental plantings of exotic conifer species, especially at Waiotapu near Rotorua, had proved highly rewarding. The Commission wrote enthusiastically of the 10 metres high radiata pines planted only 9 years previously. The report recommended that exhaustive experiments be made to test the qualities of this and other exotic timbers growing in the pumice soils.

The inquiry bore fruit. Sixty years later 405 000 hectares of this volcanic plateau is under man-made forest and not only the landscape but the economy and demography of the region has been transformed. Although not the only major industry in the region—hydro-electric and geothermal power, pastoral farming, and tourism are also very important—the forest-based industries are undoubtedly the most extensive, the most spectacular in their continuing growth, and the most lucrative. Exotic softwood forests are not confined to this region—there are large plantations in Northland, Hawkes Bay, Nelson, Canterbury, and Southland—but the pumice plateau is outstanding for the scale of its afforestation and for the profound effects which the pine tree has had upon the total pattern of wealth and activity there and around its borders.

The region, in terms of major industrial characteristics, functional interdependence, and broad demographic trends may be conveniently defined by drawing a line connecting Tauranga (and its port, Mount Maunganui) in the north-east with Putaruru and Tokoroa in the north-west, down to Taupo in the south, then to Murupara and Whakatane in the east, and back to Tauranga (see map 1). Rotorua County is central to the region while parts of 4 other counties—Tauranga, Whakatane, Taupo, and Matamata—make up the whole. Within this area we now find 2 cities—Rotorua (population 31 300)[1] and Tauranga (28 200); a large country borough—Tokoroa (15 200); and several boroughs other than cities—Mount Maunganui (8800), Te Puke (3 400), Kawerau (6 700), Whakatane (9 700), Murupara (2 800), Taupo (10 600), and Putaruru (4 600). There are also numerous small county towns, townships and settlements, some of which have been closely associated with either the indigenous or the new pine timber industry and are still.

Not all of the larger towns can be accurately described as 'timber towns'—indeed only 3 (Murupara, Kawerau, and Tokoroa) have been created exclusively to serve the industry. But all have been affected, in increased population and wealth, by the forest industry. Putaruru, once predominantly a timber town, now serves an additional important function as a farming service centre. The modern, new, deep-water port of Mount

Map 1   Central North Island Region

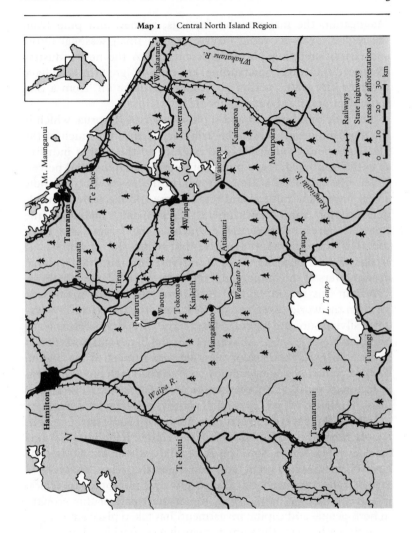

Maunganui, the major outlet for logs, timber, and pulp from the region, owes its rapid growth from a small seasonal resort and coastal shipping port almost entirely to the new industry. Tokoroa, the most outstanding example of growth, will have achieved city status within 30 years of its 'take off' from a tiny settlement of only about 200 people.

The very rapid growth and sophistication of Rotorua, which is the most important service or 'tributary' centre for much of the plateau region, is probably due as much to the timber industry as to the combined development of tourism, farming, and power. It was often dubbed a 'timber town' in the 1950s. But it is now a very important cultural and retail centre and the regional headquarters for most government departments, including the Rotorua Forest Conservancy, which is the largest and most complex territorial administrative unit of the Forest Service. It is also the national centre of forest research, and the national headquarters of the influential Timber Workers' Union are there.

Within this region we find Kaingaroa, the largest man-made forest in the world (over 121 500 hectares). It employs 1000 workers in silviculture and logging. The 2 largest wood processing companies in New Zealand—Tasman Pulp and Paper and N.Z. Forest Products—have their major plant and investment in the region. These 2 companies alone employ 7000 to 8000 men between them in factories, mills, and forests on or near the plateau. The largest plant, Kinleith, which 'created' Tokoroa, employs 3700 workers.

In 1966 there were approximately 250 000 people in the region. People from all over New Zealand, the United Kingdom, Continental Europe, North America, Australia, and the Pacific Islands have been attracted to it and consequently it has grown at a greater rate than even the fastest growing metropolitan region in the country[2]. What is more, the greatest part of this growth, in both people and capital investment, has taken place since 1945.

In the early 1920s the pumice plateau was considered one of the areas of the North Island which were least suitable for economic exploitation and human settlement. The climate is relatively harsh, with extremes of winter cold and summer heat. Pastoral farming was expanding only slowly and did not flourish until the cause of 'bush sickness' in stock animals was traced to a deficiency of cobalt in the pumice soils. Roads, even main ones, were primitive. Rotorua, the only inland settlement registered as a borough in 1926 (population 4600), depended largely on its tourist trade and its function as a service centre and railhead for many scattered bush sawmills, a few pioneer pastoral farms, and, of course, the indigenous Maori communities in the Lakes district. There were few other inland settlements of any size or economic importance. There were many mill camps and settlements, a few of which have survived to the present day and some of these have developed into towns. One is worthy of special mention because of its historic relationship to the locality which is now Tokoroa, the timber town.

Putaruru, on the north-west margin of the plateau, was a mill village and railhead (or rather, the point where the government railway ended and the private track of the Taupo Totara Timber Company began). It was also the outpost of a pioneer dairy and cattle farming community which extended southward to a tiny settlement known then as Maraetai but later as Tokoroa.

The following account from an early resident[3] tells us something of this district and the region beyond. He lived and worked at Maraetai (Tokoroa) between 1917 and 1920. His first job was to deliver a Samson tractor to the Matarawa Land Company. This had arrived in Putaruru by government train and was off-loaded to the Taupo Timber Company train which ran between Mokai, the company's own railhead and mill township near Taupo, and Putaruru. The author travelled on the same train for the fifteen mile journey to Maraetai.

I rode up to Maraetai in the little van that always travelled with the train for the convenience of passengers. Except for an area around Lichfield and a Mr Carr-Rollett's place nearer Maraetai most of the country between Putaruru and Maraetai was still in its native state.

The little Maraetai station was on the west of the line [see map 2] and comprised a store room and an open waiting room on a strong wooden platform . . .

The Matarawa Land Company had been breaking in country for at least twelve months before I arrived in the winter of 1917 and one of the first jobs the tractor did was a stationary one driving a chaff cutter and turning two stacks of oats into chaff. These oats were grown on a block of country between the railway and the main South Road, and just north of the Maraetai Road. . .

Map 2   Early sketch map of Maraetai (Tokoroa)

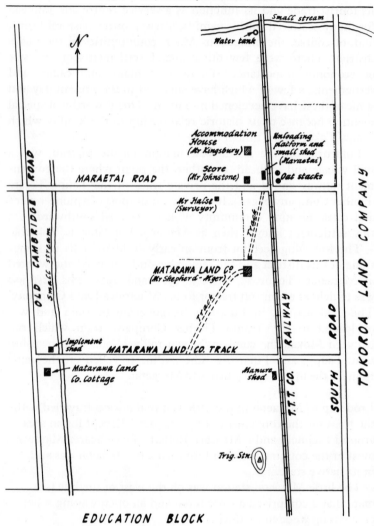

Maraetai   (Tokoroa)   1917–20
from a sketch map supplied by Mr Gordon S. Campbell

On the other side of the railway line was the General Store run by a Mr and Mrs Johnston.

Beyond Maraetai, southward, where pine plantations (some in their second generation) now flourish to feed the Kinleith Mills, the land was desolate and the roads exceedingly rough. The author takes us north from the Atiamuri bridge in the direction of Tokoroa.

Shortly after crossing the bridge there was a steep rocky left-hand turn. I might mention here that except for a row of old trees on the roadside just south of Atiamuri the only pines in this area were isolated self-sown ones, and with the exception of a few patches of native bush the hills were clothed in scrub, fern, and tu–tu[4]. These conditions prevailed to within two or three miles of where Tokoroa is now.

Just north of the Rotorua turn-off you drove down a short pumice cutting to a small bridge. Travelling up this small cutting could be difficult as the pumice sand seemed to be always dribbling down off the bank and covering the road, such as it was, and if you took it too cheaply you could come to a stand-still. Just across this little valley on a terrace there was quite a substantial dwelling situated in a fenced area that was apparently being farmed. The occupier at this time had come from Hamilton with his family and to help things along they took in travellers. Our party stayed here for the night on one occasion and we were made very comfortable. Apart from one or two dilapidated huts on the left, well back from the road near some bush, this was the only building you saw between Atiamuri and Maraetai.

There were quite a few obstacles on the road about here. The worst of these were soft patches which must have been fed by underground springs, as they never seemed to dry up properly and on occasions they could look pretty awful. They were a morass with manuka sticks protruding through the mud, apparently put there by motorists trying to extricate themselves. The procedure on coming to the worst of these patches was to stop and make an inspection, pick out what looked like the best track and then rush it as although these wet spots were fairly numerous, they were seldom more than half a chain long, and the rushing tactic generally got you through. The road wound along valleys a good deal here and at one spot you passed between two massive rock outcrops that could have been no more than ten feet apart. The floor of the valley at this point also had rocks protruding from it and you had to be careful how you straddled some of these or you could crack a crank-case or gearbox. Climbing out of this particular valley the grade steepened to 1 in 6 for a short distance as indicated by a gradient meter I had fixed to the car.

Another obstacle that looked rather formidable, especially when mounted on a motor bike, was a stream that crossed the road near where Kinleith is now. I never encountered this stream in an unfordable state but I heard of travellers being held up here.

It was somewhere near here that you first started travelling parallel with the Taupo Totara Timber Company's railway which extended from Mokai down to Putaruru. The railway line was two or three hundred yards away on your left and kept approximately this distance from the road until a hill about one mile north of the Maraetai siding forced them further apart.

This rawness of landscape was characteristic of most of the central North Island region at this time, and for the greater part of its perimeter it was, and is, bounded by rugged bush-covered ranges to the north, west, south, and south-east. But along the north-eastern margin of the plateau the land falls away abruptly to the more fertile and mild Bay of Plenty coastal plain where both European and Maori population was more numerous and small towns and settlements less widely dispersed. Tauranga, to the north, was a resort and farming service centre somewhat smaller than Rotorua. Further south, the smaller towns of Te Puke and Whakatane (also a coastal port) served a mixed economy based on dairying, flax and maize growing, and a slowly declining in-digenous timber-milling industry. All 3 towns and several smaller townships were also service centres for the numerous and steadily expanding Maori population which was dispersed in many even smaller village communities. This Maori population was to contribute much, in the following generation especially, to the development of the new timber industry further inland.

In 1920 the New Zealand Government created the Forest

Service as a separate state department 'charged with administering the forest law and ensuring that forests and their products are available for the use of all generations' (Kennedy 1951: 189). Large scale planting of pines began on the Kaingaroa plains in the mid-1920s under the direction of the Forest Service. The work continued during the Great Depression using 'unemployed' labour housed in tents and crude shacks. By 1936, 85 000 hectares had been planted in this forest alone, and small permanent settlements of Forest Service rangers and workers were established at Kaingaroa headquarters camp and in subdivisional areas of the great forest.

Meanwhile, a group of far-sighted speculators had launched extensive afforestation projects along the Waikato River north of Taupo. The largest of these ventures was to become N.Z. Forest Products Limited, a multi-million dollar company which now operates one of the two largest pulp and paper mills in the country (Kinleith) and has created the largest timber town (Tokoroa). This company tells its own story:

N.Z. Forest Products Limited was formed in 1935 to take over the forests and assets of N.Z. Perpetual Forests Limited, an afforestation company, for the purpose of commercially utilising the forests reaching maturity. N.Z. Perpetual Forests Limited was a tree planting company which sold bonds and in turn undertook to plant an acre of trees for each one sold and to maintain the planted area for a maximum of 20 years. Following the findings of a commission of enquiry, N.Z. Forest Products Limited was incorporated and the task of converting bondholdings into shares in the new company began. With the completion of the conversion, N.Z. Forest Products Limited was in possession of 176 000 acres of pine forests and some $2 694 000 in cash but no manufacturing plants[5].

The first exploitation of exotic forests in the region began at Waiotapu (Kaingaroa State Forest) in the 1920s when pit-props, posts, poles, and firewood were extracted. But the most significant development was a relatively small, unsung venture launched in 1939. The private company of Whakatane Board Mills (now owned and controlled by N.Z. Forest Products Limited) in that year produced 7 000 tonnes of cardboard from pines grown in the firm's own forest at Matahina, not far from the present site of Kawerau. It thus pioneered the pulp and paper industry in New Zealand. A feature of this company's development was one repeated later by both the larger companies referred to above; this was the recruitment of technical experts (chemists, engineers, paper-makers) from as far away as the United Kingdom, Scandinavia, and North America. For most of its labour force, however, the Board Mills was able to draw upon the population in Whakatane town and smaller surrounding communities. By 1955 this labour force had grown to 500.

A few other significant instances of capital development in the timber industry took place within the region before 1945. In 1941 a large modern State Sawmill was erected at Waipa near Rotorua, to be fed by the rapidly maturing softwoods of Whakarewarewa and Kaingaroa State Forests. A small settlement was also built to accommodate single and married workers, but some commuted, as they still do, from nearby Rotorua. Meanwhile, in 1939 a sawmill which was neither very large nor of immediate economic significance had been erected by N.Z. Forest Products Limited at Waotu, not far from the present site of Kinleith. It was an experimental plant and its full importance could only have been understood in the light of that company's burgeoning plans and investments in the timber processing industry, one of the earliest of which was the establishment of a wallboard plant at Penrose, Auckland, 3 years later. But generally the war years interrupted large-scale schemes for the development and exploitation of the region and the giant forests were barely maintained, with a reduced labour force, until the end of hostilities. The war years saw a noticeable acceleration in the growth of the few larger towns in the region (at the expense of the population in the countryside, it seems) but, overall, the population of the region showed less change in the 20 years preceding 1945 than it was to show in the 6 years following.

In the immediate post-war years, the Forest Service was the first employer in the industry to recruit labour on a large scale and from far and wide.

With buoyant economic conditions creating a keen demand for labour, (throughout New Zealand) and shortages delaying the provision of accommodation, the increase in available forest labour fell far short of expectations. Nor with competitive wage rates in industry was it possible to achieve the desired stability among such forest labour as was offering. . . . Consequently, upon the Government adopting a policy of immigration, the Forest Service made known its requirements to the immigration authorities.[6]

Two hundred United Kingdom migrants were directed to state forests in 1947 and 1948. Many went to Kaingaroa where logging operations had begun, where a second large sawmill was being completed, and where silvicultural operations were seriously behind schedule. The Kaingaroa headquarters village grew rapidly from a handful of houses and a run-down camp to become, for a time, the largest and busiest forest settlement in the land, and a prototype, in its tempo of growth and pattern of recruitment, for the larger forest towns which were to be created over the next few years. For example, among these Kaingaroa workers were the first Pacific Island migrants to the region; these were from the Cook Islands. Less typical perhaps were the Canadians, recruited to Kaingaroa in the mid-1950s. Many of these early migrants, and later ones, moved on to other logging and timber processing centres in the region.

United Kingdom migrants, especially those with families and those practising skilled trades, usually did not stop in the forests beyond the 2 year contract period. However, the most important single source of labour, in this as in other industrial settlements, were New Zealanders, Maori and Pakeha.

The early 1950s were also years of great activity in hydro-electric dam construction along the upper reaches of the Waikato River, and of land development and public works generally in the region. Dam construction alone drew many thousands of workers and the town of Mangakino (39 kilometres from Tokoroa) was built especially to house construction workers and their families. Many people, especially the young and unmarried, moved around from one industrial site to another, following the 'big money', more interesting jobs, and friends and kin, and in some cases evading creditors and the law.

In the early 1950s the forest industry was making new demands as bright prospects for export earnings were being realised. The 2 giant pulp and paper mills—Kawerau in the east and Kinleith in

the northwest were under construction. Their attendant towns and
a brand new logging town, Murupara, on the upper Rangitaiki
plain near Kaingaroa, were also being built. Kinleith (with
Tokoroa as its town) was to be self-sufficient as a centre of operations for silviculture, logging, and processing. But Kawerau is
much further from its source of supply. A 56 kilometres railway
was thus built to Murupara which became the log-loading point
and an important centre for logging operations in the great
Kaingaroa forest.

Unmarried workers, who were the most mobile and most
easily and quickly accommodated, formed the largest part of the
work force until the towns and mills were established. Continuous
demands for such a work force over the whole region gave rise to
the distinctive features of what has been called 'the age structure
of the pioneer community'—its youth and 'high masculinity'
(Franklin 1969: 67–8). Even after 20 years of growth and matura-
tion some of these features were still prominent. For example, in
the now large town of Tokoroa in 1969 we found only 37 per cent
of the adult population over 40 years of age. (The national
figure was about 57 per cent in 1966.) And, in a survey sample of
200 there were no retired persons at all (see Pitt and Swain 1970:
16). The sex ratios in mill towns and forest settlements are consist-
ently in favour of males, both Maori and European. The national
numerical advantage of males over females is less than 1 per cent,
but for Tokoroa in 1966 it was about 7 per cent, and for both
Kawerau and Murupara, 10 per cent. In both Rotorua and Tauranga, by contrast, there was a small excess of females (between
2 and 3 per cent).

As construction of homes proceeded, the proportion of married
workers and their families (usually young families) increased. But
single men's camps remain to the present time as a characteristic
of all these timber towns whether large or small. This accentuates
what is, even now, another feature of these towns and settlements
—their relatively high turnover of personnel. In Kawerau in 1961,
5 years after the mill had commenced production, Whitelaw
(1961: 79) estimated a turnover in the workforce of up to 40 per
cent (about 400 workers) over the following two years, though
admittedly not all these would be residents of either Kawerau or
nearby Onepu, but daily commuters from further afield. In
Tokoroa in 1969, 15 years after the establishment of the mill and

the town we found that 86 per cent of the householders in the sample had been resident in the town for 10 years or less, 63 per cent for only 5 years or less and 1 in every 6 had been in residence for less than 1 year (Pitt and Swain 1970:21). Even allowing for the rapid expansion of the mill, these figures would seem to imply a fairly high rate of departure as well as of arrival. Some of the consequences of both the age structure and mobility are discussed in later chapters.

Overseas European migrants—of many nationalities but predominantly British—now tend to be found in the larger towns. In Tokoroa, for example, they make up 20 to 25 per cent of the adult population. Some are skilled tradesmen and professionals attracted to this country by, among other things, brighter prospects for advancement and perhaps greater income in an industry where their skills are at a premium. But amongst these people and the less skilled there are also more varied and idiosyncratic reasons for migrating. Some wished to 'escape crowded conditions and security at the cost of freedom' (United Kingdom). Some wanted to get away from 'hard climates' (United Kingdom and Canada). Some wanted more secure all-year-round employment. Most wanted a healthier and freer environment in which to raise children. Some just had 'itchy feet' and 'wanted a change'. A few—but very few—followed kinsmen and friends.

Pacific Island people, most of them from the Cook Islands and Samoa, are dispersed over much of the region but with notable concentrations in Rotorua and Tokoroa. In Tokoroa they form approximately 12 per cent of the population. There is also a small and recently established community of Tokelauan people at Taupo where the husbands work for the Forest Service. The Pacific Island peoples have migrated largely in pursuit of higher living standards for themselves and for their children, and for kinsmen at home whom they are able to assist with gifts and remittances. They have utilized their extended family networks as information channels, as agencies for assistance in migration from homelands and recruitment to new jobs, and, when in the unfamiliar and exacting environment of the new town or settlement, as a social refuge. The rapid adaptation of these people, especially the Samoans, to industrial town life, has been a formidable achievement and a tribute to the flexibility and strength of their institutions.

Local Maoris were prominent in the indigenous timber industry on the plateau. They also formed an important, often decisive, part of the early labour force which established the new pine forests. But from 1945 Maori workers from just beyond the plateau (and, increasingly, from far beyond the region) began to outnumber local Maoris in all except the smallest and oldest forest settlements. The populations of ancestral communities from Tauranga to Opotiki along the Bay of Plenty coast and in the immediate hinterland had been growing steadily for decades. Pressure on land resources, the growing complexity of remaining land titles, and general shortage of capital for land development had long impelled Maori breadwinners to seek employment in what industries the region had supported, the working of indigenous timber resources being an early and important one. The great post-war migrations of Maori people, most spectacular in their contributions to the life of towns and cities in the North Island, but impressive also in their impact upon the small 'frontier' communities of the central North Island region, have been the result of growing social and economic pressures. There are also the positive attractions of vocational variety, the chance of incomes which allow for a wider margin of choice in consumption patterns, the prospect of home ownership, and better education for children. At first, and in some measure still, the migrations were relatively local, possibly due to a wish not to move too far from ancestral communities and more specifically, it seems, because of the more effective communication networks among kinsmen and friends which operate in and around the home locality. One of the largest developments in the forest industry in the 1950's was centred in the eastern Bay of Plenty within daily, or at the most, weekly commuting distance of many Maori home communities.

The pattern of distribution of Maoris in proportion to Europeans in the timber towns and settlements of the region is an uneven one, with contrasts as great as that between the logging town of Mürupara where Maoris outnumber Europeans by several hundred, and Tokoroa where in 1966 Maoris were only 15 per cent of the total population. This may be explained only partly by the occupational structure of the 2 towns; it is so often assumed that Maoris are 'attracted' to bush work, which in Tokoroa is only one of many occupations. An alternative explanation is that fewer Maoris found Tokoroa easily accessible when operating out of their home communities in the early 1950's and so gained less of a foothold in the place. This suggestion is supported indirectly by the evidence from Kawerau, a comparable industrial plant but one which offers no actual bush work. Yet in 1966 its Maori population was approximately 23 per cent of the total. Moreover, it seems that among the daily commuters who make up 20 per cent of the total work force, the majority have been Maoris from the many ancestral communities in the district (see Whitelaw 1961:80).

The pattern of migration and motivation to migrate amongst New Zealand Pakehas is probably more complex because of the greater range of occupations (including many professional and retail service occupations) and statuses which are represented within this category. Whatever the motivation, whether it is more money, cheaper housing, a chance to save, advancement in a career, or just adventure and novelty, the New Zealand Pakehas come from more varied and far-flung geographical regions, both urban and rural, and from more varied social and cultural backgrounds.

One might predict quite safely that the kinds of developments outlined above will continue on towards the end of the century. The region will become more populous by far, from migration as well as by natural increase. It will become more sophisticated in its technology and organization and more varied in its institutional life. It will become more urbanized, and planning will play a more important part in this as in industrial development.[6] The impersonal driving force behind all these developments is New Zealand's need to diversify away from its basically agricultural economy. Government and big business alike have enormous confidence in the future of forestry, in the saleability of wood products on the world market. Translated into the movement of capital and people, this means not only the possibility of maintaining high national living standards for some time to come, but that opportunities are being created for specific categories of people to make advances in living standards by participating directly in the industry. It means opportunities in other fields as well.

So far we have reviewed in broad outline the development of the region, with special emphasis on the movement of people following investment in productivity. In later chapters an attempt will be made to describe aspects of social capital and social investment within one timber town, Tokoroa.

NOTES

1 Round figures based on the 1971 official census. For Rotorua and Tauranga, 'city' and not 'urban area' figures were used. See *New Zealand Census of Population and Dwellings 1971, Increase and Location of Population*, vol. 1, Department of Statistics Publication, Wellington, 1972.

2 See *The New Zealand People 1966*, vol. 10 of the General Report on the *Census of Populations and Dwellings 1966*, pp. 12–13. Two statistical areas, Central Auckland and South Auckland-Bay of Plenty (into which our region falls, and to which it has contributed the largest part of its growth) exceeded by wide margins the national growth rate of 90 per cent for the years 1926–1966. The figures are 159.7 and 168.3 per cent respectively (the next highest being Wellington with 86 per cent). Rotorua city, which had grown six-fold during this period, and three-fold since 1945, had an intercensus growth rate of 34 per cent, making it one of the fastest growing urban areas in the country. The growth rate of Tauranga, with its 'twin borough' of Mount Maunganui, had also been spectacular and the trend continued into the 1966–1971 intercensus period.

3 I am indebted to Mr Gordon S. Campbell of Havelock North, for supplying first hand descriptions from which the extracts were taken, and also the accompanying sketch map of 'Maraetai'.

4 Tu-Tu: a pendulous native shrub (coriaria spp.), poisonous to stock.

5 N.Z. Forest Products Limited's brochure, *Our Industries*, 1971, p.2.

6 *N.Z. Journal of Forestry*, vol. VI, No. 1, 1949, p.2.

7 See for example, the Forestry Development Conference's *Manpower* Report, 1969, which recommends strongly that no major investment be made in the future in small forest communities but that the industry be serviced by manpower located in towns and tributary centres which offer a fairly full range of services and social and cultural amenities. (See also Chapple 1973, for a criticism of some of the assumptions of this report.)

Company and Mill 2

There are about 400 businesses of all kinds in Tokoroa, the majority employing only one or a few people in one or other of the many service industries. Only about 40 of these businesses could be classed as manufacturing—and housebuilding is included among them. Altogether, these businesses employ considerably fewer people than does a single company—N.Z. Forest Products Limited—with its forests and timber, pulp and paper mill, and its subsidiary industries such as housebuilding.

The mill, especially, is a prime fact of life for Tokoroa's 16 000 residents. It is the giant industrial plant which occupies some 200 hectares of ground, uses about 8000 tonnes of pine logs each working day, and employs 3500 workers. The original plant, officially opened early in 1954, has steadily increased its annual output of timber, pulp and paper, and other products, as new machines have been installed and it is now one of the largest of its kind in the world. Kinleith, the mill, provides the greatest part of the material wealth and well-being of the town by means of the salaries and wages earned by its employees. It determines the daily tempo and rhythm of activities not only for the workers themselves but also for their families and for a host of people in service occupations such as taxi and bus drivers, telephone operators, hotel and shop proprietors and staff. The mill and company is a career for hundreds of men and women; it is their security which stretches indefinitely into the future. Mill and work place is a daily social experience as well for most if not all employees. It is an arena and opportunity for the expression of self both on the job and during rest and leisure breaks. Employment at the mill leads also to other forms of association and activity in trade unions, clubs, and informal networks of friendship. But, above all, the mill is provider—munificent provider—of the means to live the desired life in the community beyond the workplace.

There is a legend concerning the late Sir David Henry, the

shrewd Scot who founded the company and shaped its early
development and the early development of Kinleith mill and
Tokoroa town. His Tokoroa town committee—composed partly
of company appointees and partly of elected residents—had
dared to hold a public meeting to discuss moves towards civic
government. It is said that Sir David appeared in person before
the assembly and threatened to take the mill 'elsewhere' and that
'the town would perish' if it chose to move away from the benign
paternalism of his company.

It was too late, of course, to take the mill elsewhere (or to block
the ultimate course of civic democracy for that matter), but the
simple truth was underlined: Tokoroa, its wealth and health and
bustle, *is* the mill and reflects the health, wealth, and activity of
that huge industrial plant. The mill and the company reflect,
in turn, the apparent soundness of an economic venture centred
on timber and its many products both for the domestic market and,
especially, for the export trade. The New Zealand wood product
industry is the darling child of economists and government and
N.Z. Forest Products Limited is this industry's largest and lusti-
est offspring.[1] Kinleith is the company's hardest working and
most productive son. And Tokoroa is Kinleith's domestic append-
age—the young wife, so to speak—the helpmate, delight, and
refuge from Kinleith's drudge and toil.

The mill is about 7 kilometres from the town's business and
shopping centre (see map 3), although the southward expansion
of Tokoroa, especially the development of company housing, has
now brought the town within about 3 kilometres of the industrial
site. Fumes from the chemical pulp mill now drift into residential
areas when winds blow from a southerly quarter. And billows
of smoke and steam can be seen against the southern skyline
on almost any day—a reminder that the town's existence and
prosperity is firmly under-written by the mill's annual output of
415 000 cubic metres of sawn timber, 3 500 000 square metres
of plywood, 1 500 000 litres of turpentine and oils, 389 000 tonnes
of Kraft paper pulp, and about 285 000 tonnes of paper of various
kinds. And if the townsman no longer looks up at the symbolic
pillar of smoke and steam at least he may still notice the daily
exodus of workers out of the residential areas—all within the space
of about an hour. Private motor cars, company vehicles (gang
trucks and runabouts), and chartered buses move towards the

Map 3   Tokoroa

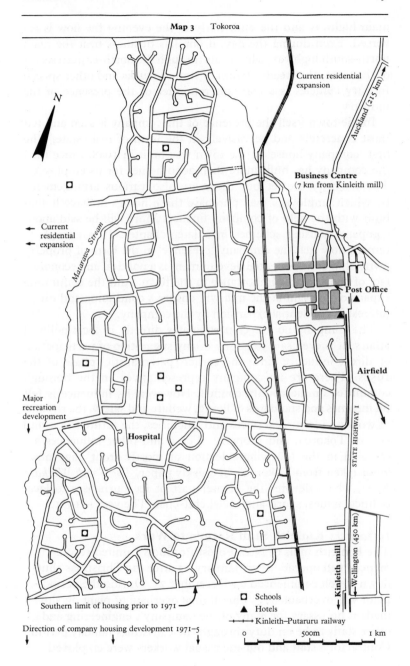

Current residential
expansion

Business Centre
(7 km from Kinleith mill)

N

← Current
← residential
← expansion

Mataraua Stream

Post Office

Airfield

Major
recreation
development

Hospital

STATE HIGHWAY 1

Auckland (215 km)

Wellington (450 km)

Kinleith mill

Southern limit of housing prior to 1971

Direction of company housing development 1971–5

☐ Schools
▲ Hotels
+—+—+ Kinleith–Putaruru railway

0   500m   1 km

main highway and the mill. Early in the evening the flow is re-
versed. Even during the day, if one has business near the main
north-south highway, which cuts through the north-eastern sector
of the town, the steady stream of timber trucks and other special
forestry vehicles is a constant reminder of the presence of the
industry.

In the town itself the presence of the company is seen and felt
most concretely and pervasively in the form of real estate. The
first 'company house' in the town was built in 1948. Since then
the company has built more than 2000 homes for its employees.
The majority are let but there are also various arrangements
by which employees may purchase these homes or have homes
built with the help of company finance. More will be said about
company housing schemes in a later chapter. It is enough to
remark now that the company 'presence' in the form of property
ownership and residential development is a political and economic
fact of considerable importance in the town. And the continuing
expansion of plant at the mill will ensure a continuing and direct
interest in residential expansion by the company.

The company no longer participates directly in local political
affairs. It is even said to be shy of any suggestion of participation
or direct influence since the earlier 'paternalistic' phase of the
1950s. There are no company representatives on the borough
committee or the county council. However, its influence is felt
on incomes and standards of living, welfare and safety, the rhythm
of work and leisure, services and amenities, the future shape and
size of Tokoroa, and property. These and other influences are
revealed in the following selection of mostly front page news
items taken from Tokoroa's bi-weekly paper, *The South Waikato
News,* which devotes the greater part of its journalism to local
political issues, sport, and social chit-chat. The year is 1971.

19 January Kinleith Staff Return to Work
The Kinleith mills of N.Z. Forest Products Limited recom-
menced full operations on January 13 after the Christmas shut-
down which commenced on December 23. During the period
plant was overhauled... This annual overhaul of plant on site
made it necessary for many of the company's engineering and
other staffs to be on duty through the Christmas holiday period.
Contractors' staff and outside casual workers were employed

during that time ... Persons in any way connected with forest
fire protection (patrols, lookouts, etc.) were of course constantly
on duty as were a large proportion of logging gangs ... with the
result that export log deliveries to Mount Maunganui and pulp
wood for local requirements were fully maintained.

26 January N.Z.F.P. Seal Arrangements for Expansion Finance

An important step in the expansion programme of N.Z. Forest
Products Limited, which will cost over $100 000 000 over the
period to 1975, was taken in Auckland yesterday when representatives of Exporters Refinance Corporation of London and
the company signed documents providing for term finance for
part of the cost of the No. 2 pulp mill and the No. 6 paper
machine, which are to be established at Kinleith. Pulp production will be doubled to 420 000 tons per annum and paper
production increased to 265 000 tons per annum.

28 January N.Z.F.P. Agrees to Meeting

The [Tokoroa Borough] committee requested that a meeting
between N.Z.F.P. heads and delegates from the committee be
held to discuss the development of Tokoroa's retail centre ...
as part of the proposed Town Plan. Land owned by N.Z.F.P.
and at present residential will have to be purchased before the
scheme can be implemented ...

16 March Company Plans Public Scenic Forest Jaunts

(Front page headlines)
Members of the public are to have the opportunity to take
scenic walks through New Zealand Forest Products Limited
owned forests. Details of the scheme and maps of the area were
presented to the Tokoroa Conservation Council recently...

18 March Company Planting Increases

Extensive planting programmes are to be carried out by N.Z.
Forest Products Ltd in the Tokoroa area, to cope with the
timber demand expected in the next 30 years.

8 April **Council Agrees to Purchase N.Z.F.P. Land**
The Tokoroa Parks and Reserves Committee . . . agreed to
recommend to the County Borough Council, that an offer from
N.Z. Forest Products Limited to sell the land adjacent to
Strathmore Park be accepted . . . The company had asked
$18 000 for the 18 acres inclusive of buildings.

4 May **New Company Airfield in Use From Today**
N.Z. Forest Products Limited's new private airstrip, south-
east of Tokoroa behind the Amisfield settlement, officially came
into use today . . . Situated only $2\frac{1}{4}$ miles by road from the
Tokoroa Post Office, the airfield nestles between two large
blocks of pine forests . . .

13 May **Realistic Income for Incapacitated Workers**
Because of the 'total inadequacy' of social security, 1000
Kinleith workers have subscribed to a group personal accident
and illness insurance scheme, launched three months ago by the
N.Z. Pulp and Paper Workers Federation.

29 June **Company Donates $1600 to Mark Safety Award**
A total of $1572 was donated by N.Z. Forest Products Limited
yesterday to 19 different charities to mark the silver safety
award presented to 'B' Shift of the paper mill at the Kinleith
site . . . There are 130 men involved in the award and their
record to date is 470 days accident free.

15 July **Strike Flares at Kinleith**
Forty-six men out following the appointment of an oilerman to
the position of charge hand . . . The union, which includes
greasers, engine drivers and firemen, want a man who they
claim to have had longer service with the company to take the
job. Company officials have refused and at midnight on Tuesday
the men stopped work. Union spokesman, Mr A. Smith, said
last night that his men have the full support of all unions
represented on the Kinleith site committee.

31 August **Kinleith Unions Agree on $9\frac{1}{2}$% Wage Increase**
Representatives of the combined unions on the Kinleith site
. . . and the company's management have agreed on new
wage and salary claims . . . The company was unwilling to

go further than the 9½ per cent claim, but the issue was finally settled by an offer of a 7 per cent bonus payment.

30 September **Turtle Club**

Mr E.G. Carlson of Tokoroa became the 19th person in the history of N.Z. Forest Products Limited to join the elite Turtle Club at a presentation on Thursday night. The club is confined to men who have been saved from serious injury or possible death by wearing a protective safety helmet.

25 November **Stoppage Costly for Company**

Last Monday's 24 hour stoppage by pulp and paper workers cost N.Z. Forest Products Limited about $450 000 in lost production. This estimate came from Sir Reginald Smythe, Chairman of the Board of Directors . . . who also estimated that the workers employed by the company would have lost about $75 000 on the stoppage. 'In the process we lost a heck of a lot of money,' he said.

A very brief sketch of the activities of the industry will enable us to appreciate the wide range of jobs and skills represented. A general description must include mention of the forest and the men who work the forest to feed the mill. Of the company's total forest assets of about 140 000 hectares, over 100 000 are located within easy reach of Kinleith. These forests of pine (Pinus radiata, a native of California) are maintained by a work force of several hundred men and youths as tree planters, pruners, and thinners. These are the silvicultural workers, or 'huhu' workers in the local idiom[2]. There are also about 200 men to whom the term 'bushmen' is more properly applied. These men fell the crop trees, trim and haul the logs, and load them onto timber trucks. Their job is exacting and often dangerous. They operate chainsaw and axe, crawler tractors or 'skyline' (overhead hauling) gear, and log-loading machinery. Overseeing the day to day work in both silviculture and logging are the leading hands and gangbosses, foremen, and forest supervisors. Then there are the foresters, professionally trained men who plan all forest operations in detail, and the men who are specially trained in the culture of tree seedlings, the forest nurserymen. There are those who make and maintain the many miles of forest roads and firebreaks, and the loading squares. And there are the fire control officers and their personnel who are charged with the ultimate safety of this multi-million dollar investment in trees. The culture and exploitation of trees is now subject to considerable scientific understanding, mechanization and control, and to complex management practices.

Over 100 timber trucks, more than half of them owned by the company, carry logs daily to the mill where a load is weighed in every 2 or 3 minutes. Giant trucks loaded with logs for export operate 'around the clock' to the deepwater port of Mount Maunganui, 105 kilometres away. There is also a continuous exodus of logs, sawn timber, pulp, and paper via government freight trains which pass day and night through the town of Tokoroa to and from their terminus and loading point at the mill. The 11 kilometres of railway sidings at the mill itself indicates the scale and complexity of this daily movement of wood and wood products. The company employs its own engine drivers and other railway personnel.

The transporting of raw material and finished products on such a grand scale, as well as the movement of men and equipment, involves the use and maintenance of many vehicles, including specialized vehicles for lifting, hauling, etc. Apart from the operators and drivers of the 500 or so wheeled vehicles of all kinds, there has to be a large staff of men to maintain these machines. Automotive mechanics and electricians, panel beaters, motor fitters, and spray painters occupy a plant which covers many hectares of the industrial site.

The major components of the mill, however, are those which have to do with the milling of logs, the treatment and storage of timber, and the manufacture of wood pulp and of paper (See figure 1). Each section employs many workers and, again, a wide variety of skills is represented.

The sawmills, timber treatment plant, drying kilns, veneer mill (for plywood manufacture), the barking and chipper mill (for the pulp mill), and timber storage yards together form a vast sprawling complex which covers about half the entire area of Kinleith. The majority of workers either operate or are 'paced' by a variety of machines; carriageways, barkers, kickers, rollers, saws, planers, chippers, conveyors, and so on, while in the timber storage yards mechanical forklifts largely replace heavy manual labour. In most areas there is loud incessant noise; in some, heat and chemical

Fig. 1 Kinleith Mill site and components

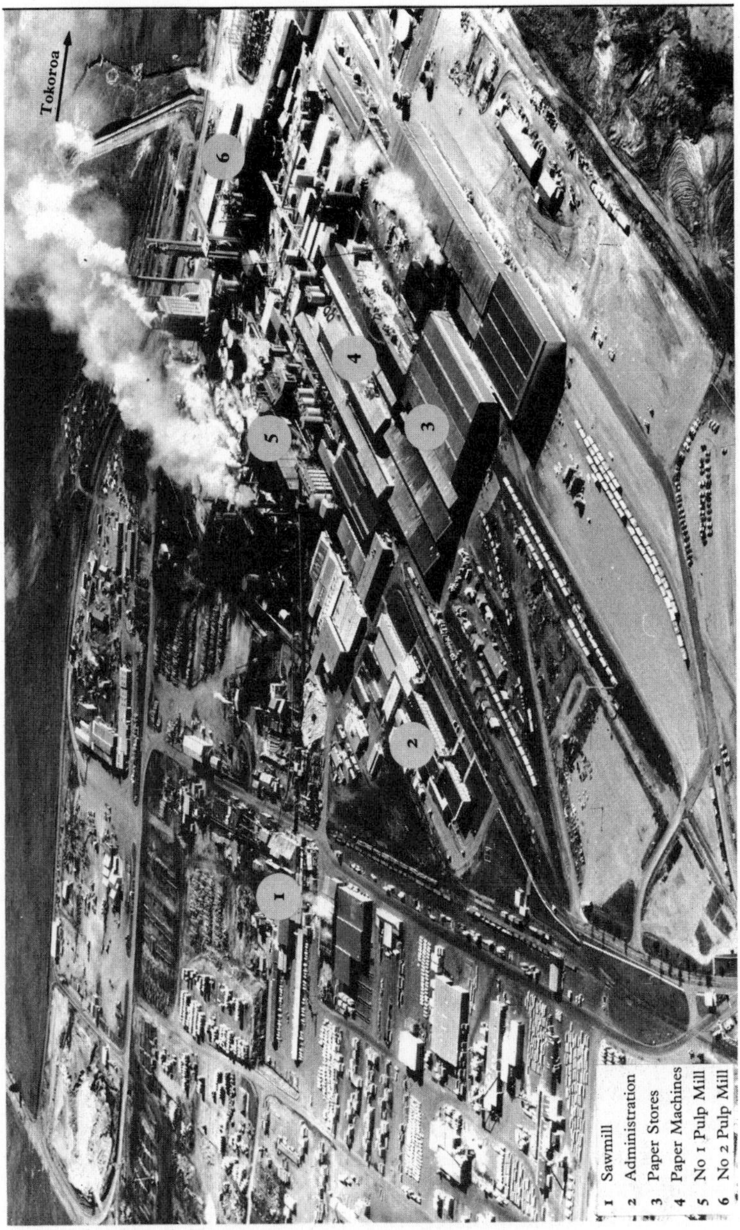
Tokoroa
1 Sawmill
2 Administration
3 Paper Stores
4 Paper Machines
5 No 1 Pulp Mill
6 No 2 Pulp Mill

fumes; and in most areas there is constant danger from machinery, logs, or moving timber.

The pulp and paper plants, with their many ancillaries (chemical and engineering servicing and by-product manufacture) together form a more compact arrangement which is more massive and generally more streamlined in its technology. These components represent the most sophisticated application of science to industry. Yet, here too, loud incessant noise, heat, or fumes are evident and danger abounds for the careless or unobservant. Wood chips from the chip mill pass by overhead conveyor into the pulp mill where they are cooked in a battery of large chemical digestors. A complex series of chemical and heat treatments follows before the pulp is ready for either export or for use in one of the 6 paper making machines in the mill itself. The whole process (or processes, for there are many) is presided over by teams of chemists, engineers, and men who have spent many years tending the machines and have an intimate practical knowledge both machine and product.

The nature of chemical pulp and paper manufacturing makes it necessary to maintain the process for 24 hours of the day, quite apart from the obvious advantages in increased output. The 3 work-shifts which this entails have the effect of promoting several subcommunities of mill employees within the main community of ordinary day-time workers. These subcommunities of shift workers have markedly different daily and weekly time and life rhythms which may affect their families also.

Forest work, log transport, vehicle maintenance, sawmilling, and pulp and paper manufacture (with supporting services) do not exhaust the inventory of activities in and around Kinleith. There are the turpentine and tall-oil plants, the box mill, a housing division (in Tokoroa), the large administrative and clerical section (employing many women), the plant fire brigade, the industrial medical service, and food catering (also employing women). Such variety has attracted not only workers seeking good wages and company benefits but also many skilled tradesmen and professionals who seek wider experience and advancement in their careers. In many fields also the company provides apprenticeships in skilled trades and cadetships in professional fields.

The processing or manufacturing components of Kinleith fall into several major categories. Each is under a management which is co-ordinated with the main administrative and decision making officers of the plant, who in turn are in close and continuous liaison with the company's headquarters office in Penrose, Auckland. The pattern is familiar. A resident director, with associate directors, translates the company's plans and policies into work and production programmes which the managers and superintendents of the various sections (forest, timber mill, pulp and paper mill, etc.,) are then charged with carrying out. The pattern has two counterpoised themes; one based upon administrative or executive authority (usually dubbed 'management'), the other based upon highly specialized technical skills—those of the engineer, chemist, or forester. Both types of role or function are carried out by salaried staff who have a 'career' in the company. The following list, taken from the public telephone directory where it appears under the company heading, indicates the higher echelons of this salaried executive and technical staff. Personal names have been omitted, leaving only the official company designation.

Mill and General
Managing Director
Director
Deputy to Technical Director
General Manager Forestry Division
Logging Manager
Assistant Logging Manager Production
Assistant Logging Manager Planning
Logging Engineers Manager
Garage Manager
General Manager Milling
Timber Sales Manager
General Manager Pulp and Paper
Deputy General Manager Pulp and Paper
Pulpmill Superintendent
Assistant Pulpmill Superintendent
Assistant Papermill Superintendent
Papermill Development Officer
Pulp and Paper Production Planning Officer
New Projects Chief Engineer
Chief Civil Engineer

Chief Operational Engineer
Branch Accountant
Branch Secretary
Personnel Superintendent
Industrial Relations Officer
Employment Officer
Purchasing Officer
Security Officer
Transport Supervisor
Building Division
Building Supervisor
Assistant Building Supervisor
Housing
Accommodation Officer
Visiting Officers
Camps
Various supervisors listed
Fire Control
Senior Fire Officer
Supervisor Fire Control
Radio Control Officer
Forestry Department
Forest Manager
Chief Inspector
Assistant Forest Manager
Nurseryman

The staff line of executive authority, which may or may not always be accompanied by a highly technical skill, extends downward in the hierarchy to the level of foreman or his equivalent. This is the lower limit of 'staff' as distinct from 'worker' status. Below this staff line one might still find supervisory roles such as gang-boss or leading hand, but one does not expect from such non-staff employees a prime loyalty to or identification with the interests of the company. Trade union membership and activity with its 'collective bargaining' strength, used from time to time against 'management' (or the company), is commonly associated with this non-staff majority of employees. And, as one might expect, the hierarchy of skills and administrative authority in the company has approximate parallels to that often vaguely-defined hierarchy of 'social classes' in the community at large—a simple but profound fact to which we will return in later chapters.

The several thousand mill and company employees have been recruited from many countries and cultures. Administrative direction is largely in the hands of Europeans—New Zealanders, Australians, and Britons. Technical direction (although it cannot always be divorced from administrative authority) is also the preserve of Europeans, though a greater variety of European nationalities tend to be represented here. Skilled (certificated) trades would seem to be represented largely by New Zealand-born Europeans (Pakehas) and British migrants, while the semi-skilled labour is supplied largely by Pakehas, New Zealand and Cook Island Maoris, and Samoan migrants. Among the non-European employees, however, there is significant representation in 'front line' (but usually non-staff) supervisory roles—notably Maoris in forest work and Pacific Islanders in the sawmill and timber yards. It appears also that young Samoan men are making a breakthrough into skilled trades.

A shared work experience 'on the floor' at Kinleith has generated at least one major recreational group in Tokoroa. The Pulp and Paper Workers' Social Association (Inc) is a social club for workers and their wives. It was opened in 1969 with 300 members and by 1971 had 1500. Its retiring secretary is a machine operator at Kinleith. He was one of a committee of 12 who began to organise for the club 5 years ago. This club, which now has fine modern premises, represents a fair cross section of the ethnically mixed working population of Tokoroa—unlike its counterpart the Tokoroa Club, which is more business and professionally aligned and is almost entirely European in membership.

There is a closer look at general occupational patterns and prospects, and the social implications of these for the community, in the next chapter. But the broad pattern of work status in the company as it affects European and Polynesian employees is indicated in figure 2 which also indicates approximately the numerical proportions (20 to 25 per cent of the employees are Maori and other Polynesian).

Fig. 2   Job status per major ethnic categories

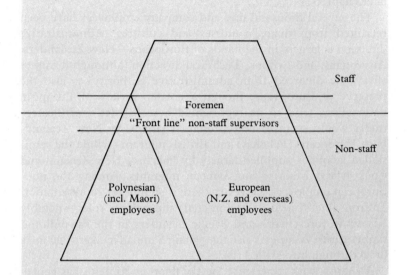

NOTES

1 'In February 1970, the company was presented with an Export Pennant and Certificate by the Rt. Hon J.R. Marshall, then Deputy Prime Minister. This award was made to the company in recognition of its outstanding achievements in the export field:' from *Outlook*—a bulletin kindly supplied by N.Z. Forest Products Limited.

2 A 'huhu' is a native wood-boring grub. The terms 'huhu' worker and 'huhu' gang appears to be mildly derogatory—denoting the generally low status of such workers in the hierarchy of skills in the forest industry.

Many Kinds of People 3

'Industry is always and everywhere a grand mixer of peoples.'
Hughes and Hughes (1952:63)

Industry in the modern world is certainly a 'grand mixer of peoples'. But what is the nature of this mixing? It does not lead quickly and easily to either genetic or to cultural sameness. Obviously the pattern of mixing will depend upon many factors: the numbers and proportions of the different kinds of people (or cultures) represented; the nature of their past cultural experiences and of the values, customs, and institutions which they bring with them to the new situation; the nature of their new experiences and of the new institutions with which they are confronted; and the prevailing attitudes of other kinds of people, especially those who tend to dominate in numbers, wealth, or influence. These would appear to be major considerations, and each will be discussed in this chapter. If the main emphasis lies in distinctions drawn between European (including New Zealand-born European or Pakeha) and Polynesian (including New Zealand Maori) it is because this is believed to be the most critically significant distinction. Problems of basic cultural adaptation—whether we think in term of 'assimilation' into or 'integration' with the mainstream of society[1]—pale into relative insignificance if we examine the record of British and other Western European migrants into New Zealand. There is nothing remarkable in this when we remember that the 'mainstream' society is European, both in numbers and in the nature of its institutions and major values. A hundred years ago, New Zealand already had a majority population of mostly United Kingdom migrants, and political and economic power had already passed into their hands. To a large extent, New Zealand became a 'little Britain of the South Seas' and, the Maori people, 'strangers in their own land'. The Europeans held the 'naming power'; it was they and not the original owners and inhabitants who were to decide on priorities and preferences (for people and behaviour as well as for things) for the next hundred years. Into this social and cultural climate Western European peoples generally, and those from the United Kingdom in particular, have been made welcome and have adapted with relative ease. Non-European people, including New Zealand's own Maori population, have not been made welcome, generally speaking. They have found it more difficult to establish a secure and comfortable place in the wider society, and seldom occupy a prestigious place. The situation in Tokoroa is modified by generally high incomes, a proportion of Polynesian peoples which is approximately double the national average (well over 20 per cent compared with about 12 per cent)[2], and a peculiarly novel and fluid style of community life. But it is not essentially altered; European language, laws, customs, and institutions prevail, Europeans still have the 'naming power'—they apportion wealth and public status to themselves and to other peoples.

Europeans of all kinds form about 75 per cent of the total population of Tokoroa—a proportion which may be diminishing owing to higher natural increase rates among the non-European groups and a possible lower rate of in-migration for Europeans. This chapter examines only the major European categories— New Zealand Pakeha, United Kingdom migrants, and the Dutch. There are many other European cultures and nationalities represented in Tokoroa, but in relatively small or very small numbers: German-speaking Swiss; Scandinavians (mostly Swedish and Danish) and Finns; Poles and other Eastern Europeans; Canadians; Yugoslavs; and probably a dozen others as well.

Approximately 2 out of 3 of the Europeans are New Zealanders by birth or upbringing. These, the Pakeha, have been migrating into the district from many parts of New Zealand since before the 1920s. First as farmers and farm workers, then as tree planters, later as forest and mill-workers and managers, until finally they came to the new town of Tokoroa in almost every occupational capacity from top-ranking company executive to the most humble labourer. They are prominent in all the professions, both in industry and the social services. They still dominate the teaching profession and tend to predominate in commercial and clerical occupations, both as proprietors and as wage and salary earners. But they are also prominent in skilled and semiskilled trades, and in a variety of unskilled occupations. In occupation, educational attainment, and life-style (cultural interests, tastes, consumer habits, and joining habits) the New Zealand Pakeha is unremarkable because so diverse—representing so many minor combinations that he cannot be clearly identified with any. Perhaps only his speech is distinctive, and that largely by default, for it is marked by no distinct brogue or twang even if it can be associated with certain colloquial expressions (and these with certain minor social mannerisms). To the recent European immigrant the New Zealand Pakeha is regarded variously as 'friendly', 'approachable', 'reserved', 'conservative', or 'cold'—which again suggests that there is no particularly distinctive New Zealand Pakeha attitude to the stranger. Between New Zealand Pakeha and Maori people there is, generally, a mutual reticence or reserve (and even mistrust) which, many would say, has been maintained largely from the Pakeha side since the earliest years of contact in the nineteenth century. It remains to this day, in Tokoroa as elsewhere, although there are notable exceptions. A similar reserve exists between Pakehas and other Polynesians. But it is by no means certain that recent European migrants enjoy easier and more cordial relations with Maori and other Polynesian people. At least this would be a doubtful claim for the United Kingdom migrants. So, even on this score the New Zealand Pakeha is not outstanding.

People from the United Kingdom form the great majority of overseas European migrants, in Tokoroa as in New Zealand as a whole. They include Scots, English, Irish, and a few Welsh. A very rough estimate of the adult population in this category would be between 15 and 18 per cent or about 1 in 6 of the adult population of Tokoroa. As selected assisted migrants many brought trade skills which they continue to practice in local industries. Professional occupations in industry and the social services are also well represented among the United Kingdom migrants; special attempts have been made from time to time, by government and local body agencies as well as by the major industrial organizations, to recruit teachers, doctors, and engineers from Britain. It seems likely, but not certain, that British migrants are rather under-represented in unskilled occupations and in private commerce in the town.

The United Kingdom contribution is considerable but it is not distinctive. There are no clubs or societies which serve the special needs of these people or reflect their recent national background.[3] Rather, they have infused a variety of club and cultural activities with their diverse interests and skills.

One special area in which the unique contribution of United Kingdom migrants is often recognized is the trade union movement. They bring a level of experience and consciousness which is unique on New Zealand's expanding industrial scene. Tokoroa exemplifies this. Of the dozen or so trade unions represented at the mill alone, one, that of the pulp and paper workers, stands out as a paragon of power and efficiency—and an Englishman stands behind it.

Mr P.J. settled in New Zealand soon after World War II, after serving for several years in the British merchant navy, where the long hours, poor pay, and substandard conditions helped to kindle his interest in trade unionism. During the bitter confrontation between waterside workers and government in 1951, he assisted in the publication of workers' underground leaflets and in other strike activities. But, when the 'new order' of compliant unionism was established on the waterfront, P.J. moved north to another field of employment—the forest utilisation industry. Soon after starting at the Whakatane mills in 1953 he was elected union delegate by the sawmill workers, and a few years later, having transferred to the pulp and paper making side, he became Branch Secretary of the union there. By the early 1960s he had moved to Auckland and the N.Z. Forest Products Limited plant at Penrose, where he was almost immediately elected Branch Secretary.

At this time the pulp and paper workers were chafing under the conciliation and arbitration system which they considered prevented them from gaining a greater share of the fruits of a highly profitable industry. P.J. took a leading part in the move to voluntary de-registration of the union, an extreme and possibly hazardous move in those days. This break from the conciliation and arbitration legislation led to massive gains by pulp and paper industry workers; at one critical point of the struggle a vital (legal) strike ballot was held at the Penrose branch of the union by the Labour Department, and when this was carried by a massive majority, N.Z. Forest Products capitulated.

By 1968 the large Kinleith branch of the pulp and paper workers union had accepted the need for a fulltime secretary for

the first time, and P.J. was selected for this post, becoming
National Secretary of the union the following year. This union has
the largest active membership, produces its own monthly broad-
sheet, and enjoys frank communication both among its members
and with the management at the mill. It has been instrumental
in obtaining a more adequate housing policy for mill workers and
in establishing, with company help, a range of recreational and
welfare services. The union has even won an informal but
effective right to advise management on promotions up to the
level of foreman. Behind much of this record of successful
unionism lies the efforts and insights of P.J. who, like so many of
his countrymen, has brought to this country an experience which
is significantly different from that developed here over a 75 year
period of mixed government protection and tight control of
industrial relations.

United Kingdom migrants enjoy, from the moment of their
arrival in New Zealand, a fairly complete familiarity with the
language of everyday life and the values and categories of thought
which underly this language. They find, too, broadly similar legal,
commercial, and educational institutions. Their problems are
likely to be personal in idiosyncratic ways. Homesickness for close
relatives and friends perhaps, or some dissatisfaction with the
paucity of certain social services or recreational and cultural
fàcilities which they may have enjoyed 'back home'; perhaps small
irritations with being required to live and work not only with
their colonial cousins but also with fellow migrants from non-
English speaking countries, with various Pacific Island people,
and with Maoris. Their new experience of people and customs is,
at least for a time, not well-ordered or predictable. But, just as the
occupational class and general cultural background of United
Kingdom migrants is very varied, so too are the individual
responses to life in the new environment. It would be futile to
generalize further about this category of people.

The next most numerous European people are the Dutch who
form very approximately 1 in 20 of the adult population of the
town. Migrating to this country mainly during the 1950s, these
people encountered initial language difficulties which were
quickly surmounted, leaving little or no trace of linguistic limi-
tations among their children who were born in New Zealand. The
Dutch, whether from Holland or Indonesia, had benefited from a

generally high formal education. They brought technical, agricultural, and commercial skills which were highly relevant to their new experience, and their generally rapid and successful adaptation to New Zealand society is proverbial. Indeed, the apparent material success of the Dutch has even given rise to some mild prejudice against the migrating generation—that they are, or were, calculating and opportunist.

One could compile an impressive list of 'success stories' for New Zealand Dutch migrants and the Tokoroa scene would provide several good examples. One will suffice. Mr. T.P. arrived in New Zealand 22 years ago from Holland where he had worked on his family's small farm. He was encouraged to emigrate, to 'do better', by a friend who had already settled in New Zealand. At first T.P. worked on a dairy farm near Auckland but soon he moved into the timber country, working in mills and factories where more money could be saved. Meanwhile, his fiancee had migrated from Holland to join him. They were married and went sharemilking for a while before moving to Tokoroa in the mid-1950s. T.P. worked in the paper mill for a couple of years and also took a milk delivery round as a sideline. In 1963 he opened a real estate business—dealing mainly in town properties—but kept his milk round. By 1971 he was able to build a two-storied business block in the bustling heart of the town. His ambition, determination, hard work, and business acumen provide a model of the work ethic and success ideal which lie at the heart of material progress and prosperity in any Western capitalist society.

In and around Tokoroa the original Dutch migrants are represented in a wide range of occupations from semiskilled labouring (probably a very small minority), through skilled trades, professions, agriculture, and commerce. The distinguishing marks of this first generation are the Dutch accent and sometimes the Dutch surname; few non-Dutch would presume to be able to identify these people by their physical appearance or their general behaviour.

Initially, and in some situations such as construction camps, the new migrant might have been characterized by a degree of 'clanishness', but although this might still be true of some Indonesian Dutch in the cities, this generalization has lost its power as the migrants have dispersed into many varied milieux in town and country. They cannot now be characterized in this way, in Tokoroa or elsewhere. And intermarriage with English speaking Europeans, especially Dutch males with New Zealand Pakeha women, has been relatively common.

There are Dutch national or cultural associations in New Zealand; Tokoroa has its branch of the Netherlands Oranje Society and Saint Nicolas' Day is an occasion for a small, colourful parade. Dutch artifacts are common in the homes of these people and visits to Holland and visits of home kin to their Tokoroa relations are quite commonplace. These are all understandable expressions of national, cultural, and kinship sentiment. But they are not, it is suggested, strategic in terms of the social and psychological adjustment of these migrants—not as similar behaviours and institutions are for Polynesian migrants.

New Zealand Maori, Cook Island Maori, and Samoan migrants, with a handful of representatives from each of several other Pacific island cultures (notably Niue, Tonga, and Fiji), together comprise over 20 per cent of the adult population of the town. With their children they may form as much as 33 per cent of the total population. The characteristic values and life-styles of these peoples, especially the migrating generation, have been shaped in environments markedly different to those of the Europeans. The cultural styles of each differ considerably among themselves, the New Zealand Maori people displaying the widest diversity in regional background and past experience with Pakeha society. Nevertheless, certain general features emerge which are common to all or most Polynesian people whether they are from small rural communities in New Zealand or from island village communities in the Cook group or Samoa. These are historical and cultural and their significance is profound. First, there has been their experience of a traditional social order based upon kinship with its hierarchy of status or rank and its widely ramified pattern of rights and obligations. Second, there are their languages (all closely related in structure and vocabulary) which embody ways of perceiving and evaluating experience which have been and still are Polynesian and not European in content; and these languages or their influences have persisted even amongst New Zealand Maoris of this parent generation. Third, there is the fact of 150 years of contact with English speaking Europeans who, from Samoa to New Zealand, came to exercise political and commercial domination wherever the two peoples met. Finally, there has been a fundamental cultural difference between Polynesian and European in the criteria of 'success' and 'the measure of a man', and in this difference lies a considerable drama which is still being worked out wherever the groups and communities of one face the communities and institutions of the other.

New Zealand Maoris have been represented in Tokoroa and the district since the earliest days of industry and settlement, not as tangata whenua (people with ancestral affiliation to the land), for there was no tribal community in the district, but as migrants from other regions, attracted by wage-earning opportunities in land development, forest, and sawmill. We have already examined the background features of this movement in Chapter 1. Their contribution to the development of the forests and the sawmilling industry is almost certainly a very important one. Photographs of road construction gangs in the district from the mid-1920s to the 1930s suggest that Maori men were numerically prominent, even though Pakehas were probably in the majority.

There are still several Maori residents living in Tokoroa who moved into the district in those early days. One is Mr D.P. who worked for the original forest investment organization, Perpetual Forests. He lived with and worked alongside New Zealanders, Maori and Pakeha, for 10 years or more, making roads and helping to establish the forests. After a couple of years away from the district he returned with his wife, who is also a Maori. That was 30 years ago when settlement in the district was small and scattered and living conditions relatively rough. Later, when the mill was established at Kinleith, D.P. obtained work in the vehicle maintenance section and thus worked for the company until his retirement in 1972. He and his wife contributed much to community life over the years by participating fully in sporting and cultural associations. Mrs P. founded the local branch of the Maori Womens' Welfare League in 1958, and, with her husband and a group of other Maori residents, established also the main Maori intertribal marae and community centre, 'Nga Waka' (the tribal canoes of the original migration). This became, in her words, 'a home away from home for many of the boys who came here'—that is for the many young Maoris who came from various tribal regions to seek work in the forest and mill.

Although Maoris were not well represented in skilled technical trades, and hardly represented at all in the professions and in commerce, they have at least since the 1940s been prominent in silvicultural work, log extraction, timber milling, building construction, transport, and road works. This pattern of occupation persists, although increasing numbers of young Maoris are becoming machine operators or work supervisors especially in the forest, and some are entering skilled trades.

The districts of origin are various, with a fairly heavy representation from Northland, many of whom followed kinsmen in 'chain migration' not unlike the pattern of migration of people from the Cook Islands (see below). But the Maori population in Tokoroa is characterized by its heterogeneity—in districts of origin, occupation, educational standards, life-styles, and patterns of intermarriage (with Maori, including Cook Island, partners predominating but marriage with Europeans is quite common).

There are also marked differences in degrees of confidence in dealing with Europeans and in the ease with which they can 'mix' socially with Europeans. It is therefore becoming almost as meaningless to generalize about New Zealand Maoris as it is about Pakehas. However the consciousness of being Maori is probably one valid generalization. Even a person who has only one Maori grandparent is likely to regard himself or herself as Maori. And, it is also likely that he or she will express this 'Maoriness' in significant ways. It may be in the maintenance of a wider network of kin than would be usual for a European person. It may mean feeling an obligation to attend certain Maori ceremonial functions (especially the tangi or funeral) as occasions arise. It is likely to mean a preference for the informal social company of other Maoris, or for Maori food and cooking methods. It is less likely to mean a full command of the Maori language but is likely to be manifested in certain mannerisms of speech, styles of humour, and interests. All this is as apparent in Tokoroa as it is wherever Maori people are dispersed amongst Europeans.

And in Tokoroa the Maori people are literally dispersed, though with a relative absence in the newer, privately financed, and more expensive residential areas and a relatively heavy concentration in the older, rented housing 'estates' of the Hutt Timber Company and the early utilitarian dwellings built by N.Z. Forest Products during their first phase of expansion. The same pattern is true for the Cook Island Maori people, and there are also concentrations of New Zealand and Cook Island Maori youths and men in the several camps or hostels operated by the company.

The pattern of joining shows a preference for certain sporting clubs—notably Rugby and Rugby League for men and netball and hockey for women—but Maori people, especially the young people, are also fairly well represented in a wide range of sporting clubs from tennis to marching girls. A few of these sporting clubs are 'ethnic' in both membership and designation, and there are other forms of association, like Nga Waka and the Maori Womens' League which are also specifically ethnic. The same is true for the Pacific Island groups (see Chapters 4 and 8 for further descriptions of ethnic clubs and associations). Maori representation in local body affairs has been good—thanks to local Labour Party encouragement, it seems—but this cannot be taken as an indication that Maoris, any more than any other ethnic or national group, are 'civic minded' in their new town environment. Indeed, Maori and other Polynesian people have rather less reason than Europeans to be 'civic minded'. This question will be raised again towards the end of this chapter. But the graphic testimony which follows anticipates the argument, and gives us further insights into those subtle differences which still distinguish Maori from European. Mrs A.R. is married to a European. She is in fact 'civic minded' and is active in a range of community affairs not all of which are concerned specifically with Maori people. She is speaking to a largely European audience at a community study 'workshop'.[4]

I want to speak on the point of view of Maori family ties, and strong tribal affiliations. If you were to come from, say, north of Whangarei (Ngapuhi) you would find all the members of that tribe and thereon up north are related somehow or other but are different again from the Waikato Maoris and even Maoris who come from further down south. Being dependent on family ties and living in a community, we have always felt we have somebody we could go to if we have any problems and can go and ask for advice—if the kids are making us climb the walls there is always some relation we can go and dump them on and go and have a holiday. Here I have nobody I can leave the children with and nobody to go to except a friend of mine and my sister-in-law. Also, we are so used to having old people tell us what to do, and if the kids get sick, we go to somebody else not the doctor—grandmother, mother, auntie, or somebody

like that. Even with Maoris there is a distinction between
Ngapuhi Maoris, Waikato Maoris, and even other tribes. Our
language is different from that of the Waikato Maoris. I also
think the reason that a lot of Maoris will not come here [that is,
to a meeting such as this] is that they don't like being laughed
at, particularly by the Pakeha; they don't like talking in front
of you—not unless there is a whole group of Maoris.

The Cook Island people are the next most important numerically. Estimates of their population vary considerably. In 1970 a
leading member of the local Cook Island community suggested
'possibly 1 000 counting adults as well as children'. Towards the
end of 1972, the Department of Maori and Island Affairs estimated
that the Cook Island community in Tokoroa stood between 1500
and 2 000 men, women, and children. Even an accurate assessment
may have to be qualified by a three figure addition, annually,
to accommodate natural increase and in-migration. The first
migrants arrived as the Kinleith mill was about to begin production. These were the trail-blazers for a community which has
become more numerous and permanent than even the people
themselves could have envisaged. One of these original migrants
tells his story:

As a Cook Islander I came with no knowledge of what was
awaiting me. My only hope in coming here was to earn enough
to go back home and live a comfortable life—not that the life
there is uncomfortable. But when I came here in the early days
of Tokoroa—when there were about 2 000 to 3 000 people, about
17 years ago—the Island community was small and I was the
third to come here and we sent word home to come—this is the
life, come!

The first Cook Island migrants came from Aitutaki in the early
1950s. People from that Island were soon so numerous in Tokoroa
that it was dubbed by the people themselves 'little Aitutaki'.
Groups bound by ties of kinship and marriage were soon established or re-established in the town. A similar process began later
with people from the island of Mangaia. It is said that these
communites of origin remain as criteria of distinction amongst the
people themselves, even though they are all, culturally, very closely

related. A third category, those from Rarotonga, tend to be less distinct because they are often spouses of the other two through marriage contracted as the outer island people lived for a time in Rarotonga as a step or stage towards migration to New Zealand. The personal dynamics of 'chain migration' (migration effected through kinship links, with kinship encouragement and assistance) and the motivation, means, and some results of it, are clearly revealed in the following extracts taken from E.M.K. Douglas's intensive study of the Tokoroa Cook Island community in the mid-1960s (see Douglas 1965: Appendix II):

When I left home I had lots of big ideas of what I was going to do in New Zealand. I was going to save hard, and send some money home to build a decent house for my mother because we lived in a kikau shack, and I was going to come back to Aitutaki and get a job. When I arrived in Tokoroa I stayed with my Auntie Tangi and Tata for a while, but then I went to live in Hillcrest camp because they were in a company house, and you're not supposed to have relations staying with you. I didn't like it in the camp because there was so much more to do in town, and when Tangi and Tata went to Hamilton to live I left the camp and I went to live with my cousin, Takao and her husband Barry. Barry is a Papa'a, [European] but I like him because he speaks the Island language. When I first arrived in Tokoroa I got a job on the Wet Tables at the Mill. The leading hand down there was a man from our village, and he had been there for a long time, and there were lots of Cook Islanders working down there then, there's even more now. There were a few Maoris and a few Papa'a working down there when I started but nowadays they are all Islanders. Well, we got plenty of overtime there and I worked as much as I could because I had to pay back my Auntie for the tickets, so I saved money and I paid her back, and then my brother Pona who was in Rarotonga being a carpenter, wrote to me to say that he wanted to come to New Zealand because he wasn't earning enough money in Rarotonga. He wanted to get married. I saved up some more money and I sent him enough for his ticket to come over here. He came and started work on the Wet Tables too.

A 32 year old Cook Island man (a relative of the first) describes his experiences ...

When Tata asked me in a letter if I'd like to come to New
Zealand, I jumped at the chance, although he made a few
conditions. He said first of all I had to come to Tokoroa to live
and stay in the camp, secondly I had to pay the money back
within a year and thirdly I had to send money back to the Cook
Islands. Well, I was 25 by that time and I had some sense of
responsibility and so I agreed to do these things. I was so keen
to come that I would have agreed to do anything. When I got
here, (that was 1957) there were by then quite a few Cook
Islanders here, some of them had moved out of Company
houses and had built their own. I think David Junior and
Catherine were the first ones to build their own house, but they
were soon followed by others until there were parts of town
where every second house was owned by a Cook Islander. When
I came to Tokoroa my cousin Jim arranged a job for me where
he worked on the No. 2 Dry Table. He hadn't been there very
long before they made him a machine operator. Now he's a
leading hand on one shift, and Tuapou is the leading hand on
the other shift . . . We find it best to work with friends or
relations from the Cook Islands. At the Dry Tables, on our
shift, the leading hand is my cousin and I have 2 other cousins
working. There are 2 other boys from Aitutaki and 2 boys from
Mangaia. On Tuapou's shift, 4 of the 8 are from Oire village
and the other 4 are from the Cook Islands. In some of the other
departments at the mill most of the boys are from Mangaia and
they group together for the same reasons.

The immediate individual motives for migrating (for Pacific
Island people in general) were various even if the underlying
pressure was the economic one—the inadequacy of a subsistence
and small cash economy to support a growing population and to
meet the rising expectations of the young for education, more
stimulating experiences, and less manual drudgery. During the
early years of settlement in Tokoroa the migrants were nearly all
young men, about half of whom were married (though these did
not necessarily, or at first, bring their wives). As the movement
gained momentum a wider range of ages was represented, and the
female proportion grew steadily. Old people have tended to come
later, as dependants of well established family groups in the town.
The children born to Cook Island couples (or spouses, for some

have married New Zealand Maoris and even Europeans) since their arrival in Tokoroa, probably now outnumber the migrants themselves.

The occupational pattern for Cook Islanders in Tokoroa stands in some contrast to the pattern for the whole town (see figure 3). Tokoroa seems to have attracted fewer skilled and professional people—most of whom, among original migrants, were trained in Rarotonga. These latter have tended to settle in larger towns and cities, especially Auckland. Adults migrating to Tokoroa have been less well prepared, educationally and vocationally, to make a breakthrough into a wider range of occupations. Their dilemma is similar to that of New Zealand Maoris but has proportionately fewer notable exceptions.

Cook Island Maoris are much closer culturally to New Zealand Maoris than they are to Samoans. Much of their language, which is represented by several' dialect forms, is immediately intelligible to a speaker of New Zealand Maori, whereas Samoan speech is largely unintelligible to both Maori language groups. But, like Samoan, the Cook Island Maori language is nearly always used in the home, in the work place where speakers are workmates, and wherever the adult generation gathers socially. (This is much less true of the New Zealand Maori.) New Zealand born children of Cook Island people understand their parents speech although the tendency has been for them to reply in the English they learn at school and use amongst their playmates. (Children of New Zealand Maori speakers are far less likely to understand their parents when they use Maori; Samoan children, on the other hand, probably have a much greater facility to speak as well as understand their ancestral tongue.) In both Cook Island and Samoan peoples' homes the material evidence of their Pacific Island origins is usually displayed in a variety of artifacts such as fans, shell necklaces, pandanus mats, and ornamented bark cloth (tapa). Adults, especially the older ones, often prefer to sit on the floor when relaxing or doing handwork. And food preferences, in kinds of food as well as methods of preparation, still tend to follow the island experience. Main meals, in Cook Island and Samoan households are usually quite distinctive; in New Zealand Maori homes, less so. Yet, in spite of the manifest or overt similarities between Cook Island and Samoan peoples—a similarity which allows the Europeans to refer to them all in popular

Fig. 3   Occupational patterns—major ethnic categories compared

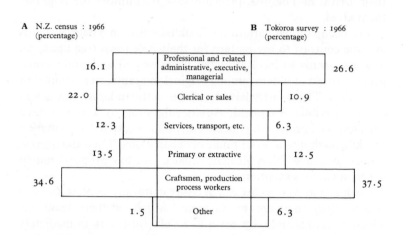

A   N.Z. census : 1966
(percentage)

B   Tokoroa survey : 1966
(percentage)

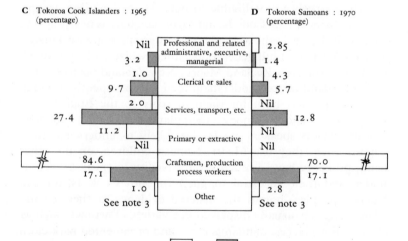

C   Tokoroa Cook Islanders : 1965
(percentage)

D   Tokoroa Samoans : 1970
(percentage)

Male   Female

speech as 'Islanders'—the similarity is superficial compared with the real cultural affinity of the Cook Island people with the New Zealand Maoris, especially with those of the latter who have retained the Maori language and life-styles.

The Samoan people of Tokoroa are the smallest, numerically, of the 3 major Polynesian ethnic groups. The estimated 500 (men, women, and children) comprise somewhat less than 3 per cent of the total population. The Samoans gathered in strength of numbers in the town, from the early 1960s. The pattern of migration has been broadly similar to that of the Cook Island people. Representatives of 'āiga or extended family groups (dispersed in New Zealand and in Western Samoan) established themselves in the town and became focal points for the reuniting of 'āiga members. The 'āiga is even more important for adult Samoans migrating directly from their homeland than the kinship group is for Cook Island people because entry regulations for Samoans are more stringent. A Cook Islander can come and go freely because he is a N.Z. citizen; a Samoan must have someone to sponsor him for employment and accommodation. The 'āiga appears to exercise considerable control both in its selection of new members which it is prepared to assist in migration and over the behaviour of its members once they are united in the new environment.[5] This 'āiga sentiment, discipline, and solidarity imparts to the Samoan community in Tokoroa some of the characteristics which are reminiscent of overseas Chinese families. The similarity is even more pronounced when we notice that the traditional cultural identity of these Samoans is remarkably well preserved in language and day to day customs and life styles, especially in their homes. There is, too, a major cultural focus in the church (usually Pacific Island Congregational or Catholic). This further encourages a personal and social morality that led one European woman in Tokoroa to exclaim that her Samoan neighbours embarrass her because 'they are more like us than we are!' She was referring to the sobriety, reserve, and decorum with which they conduct themselves in public.

At present, the Samoan people tend to be the most isolated and socially and culturally distinct even though they are well-dispersed residentially. And they seem to have even less social discourse with other Polynesian groups than they do with Europeans, if the pattern of 'intermarriage' is any indication. Pitt and

Macpherson (1971: 49–50) found that approximately 1 in 5 persons in Tokoroa and in Auckland had either 'intermarried' or had immediate relatives who had done so. In both the Tokoroa and the Auckland samples, Maori and 'other Pacific Islander' as marriage partners, were heavily outnumbered by European spouses.

This relative cultural isolation, with strong family organization and an extra-familial focus in the church, may in fact be a long term asset for the Samoan people in Tokoroa. It may be that they, to a greater extent than either the New Zealand or Cook Island Maori people, will be able to 'bargain' or lay down the terms of their place in the community as a whole. They already have a slight advantage over the Cook Island people in occupations (see figure 3). And at least locally, Samoans enjoy an enviable record among the Polynesian groups for 'keeping out of trouble'.[6] Although at least half of the adult migrants look back to their homeland, hoping or intending one day to return, the great majority will in fact remain (though not necessarily all in Tokoroa). Their New Zealand-born children will not feel quite the same 'homeward' pull. They are already bi-cultural to a more profound extent than are their parents. And one would hope that for several generations at least these people could remain bi-cultural, moving with increasing ease and confidence in the society at large but operating out of the rich, distinctive, and strong cultural base of fa'a samoa—the Samoan way.

Before drawing in the threads of this chapter it would seem fruitful to obtain a glimpse of attitudes which some residents maintain towards the 'many kinds of people'. I have chosen as a source the casual ethnographic observations obtained by interviewers during the university survey of the town in November 1969. (As one of each pair of interviewers questioned each individual or couple, the other recorded a variety of information including significant asides in conversation). The majority of these make no specific reference to ethnic relationships. But from several dozen which do I have culled the following mixed bag and have attempted to arrange them in three classes in order of attitude, from crude negative prejudice to some evidence that the respondent appreciates the cultural 'other' or in some way believes in or has experienced the ideal of tolerance and social exchange in spite of cultural differences. Unfortunately, the material from the Polynesian side is sparse. Not only were there very few Polynesians in the sample but few, if any, pronounced upon their relationships with or attitudes to Europeans—which is perfectly understandable in the circumstances. However, it is perhaps more appropriate that attitudes from the dominant (that is European) category should be our major concern; they would seem potentially the more destructive of human relationships. And we are not concerned, primarily, with the truth or fallacy of the statements, or with any quantitative assessment of types of attitudes; we use the material to obtain insight into the variety of attitudes and experience of residents.

A woman school teacher who had spent many years in Tokoroa for the sake of her husband's job does not like the area or the neighbours because there are 'a lot of Maoris and Islanders'. Another younger married woman who works as a receptionist and doesn't much like living in the town said 'I wouldn't live in— Street; too many Maoris'. A 40-year-old housewife complained that she and her husband would not have bought the section on which they had built their home had they known there were going to be Maoris in the area. This 'lowered its value' for them. She also remarked upon 'those Maori children next door; you bar your children from playing there and they come over to your house!'. A middle-aged migrant, a security patrolman, sees the mixed races as a source of trouble and, about 'Maoris and Islanders' he declared: 'Drink goes to their head ... The only way they feel things is through their pocket so slap the fines up.' And, describing 'Islanders': 'Life's just one long time of playing the guitar and drinking beer. They don't care much about the kids.' An Englishman, whose family has grown up and left the town suggested that 'Maoris and Islanders should conglomerate' to form a kind of ghetto; that they 'create problems for themselves' (under the present residential pattern, presumably) 'by their communal living'. He thinks Tokoroa is a 'difficult town to live in' because of the 'races' and supports the South African and Rhodesian solution. He also criticised 'the Islanders' for remitting so much money to the islands, and for spending the rest on the 'T.A.B., chain stores, and the pub'.

This class of statements is the bluntest, crudest, or most extreme. The next class reveals at least a little more thought and concern for the other party.

A young Pakeha husband, university trained, believes that it is necessary to provide 'guidance' for 'Islanders' because trouble and racial strife arise through their ignorance of local social customs. Another older man, a Canadian, also feels that 'Islanders come here unprepared'. A young mother was concerned about the 'poor English' of Island people, and mentioned also that there was prejudice between Maoris and Islanders (whom the Maoris call 'coconuts') and even between different groups of Islanders. She said Maori and Island mothers 'do not think of putting their children on a list for kindergarten' until too late, thereby often missing out. The wife of a man prominent in civic affairs offers a somewhat backhanded compliment to 'Islanders'. She sees them performing a twofold vital service to the community, 'keeping the money spinning by big spending' and, by doing 'vital work', by which she meant necessary work which not many other people would want to do. A Southern European woman, married to a Scots migrant, testified that she was scared of unintentionally offending people of other ethnic groups by some remark or action which had different implications in their culture, and that she felt this as a barrier to 'intermingling'. She felt especially the 'large gap between the two cultures', in this case, 'Islander' and 'European'. A Pakeha tradesman only 8 months resident in Tokoroa described much the same phenomenon when he commented briefly upon his Samoan neighbours, 'They say hello but keep to themselves'. An elderly couple, who had spent more years in Rotorua than in Tokoroa, said that although they 'liked Maoris', they felt that 'Islanders were a problem'. And a middle-aged Scots wife who has spent most of her 23 years in New Zealand in Tokoroa, still finds that she 'can't get through to them' (Islanders) even though she has tried to be friendly. She believes that they 'don't try to adjust to New Zealand ways of living' and they appear to make very little contact with Europeans.

Finally we come to that class of remarks which reveal, for all their variety, a unifying theme. This is the ideal (implied rather than stated) that, whatever the problems or difficulties encountered among the various ethnic groups, the community is, or ought to be, free of any prejudice or discrimination. The fact that there are fewer examples to draw from may be significant in assessing the amount of such essential goodwill in the community.

A Canadian migrant, a married woman living in a neighbour-hood in which there are many Maori families, feels that the company housing policy is excessively restrictive towards Polynes-ian families and does not take into account their special needs. She has also stopped attending her particular church because the congregation reflects the snobbish indifference of a European 'executive class'. 'If a Maori family living down the road needed assistance,' she declared, 'these so-called Christians would do little if anything to help them'. Another woman, a voluntary social worker and wife of a company accountant, cited manifestations of the 'class and race prejudice' which, she maintains, exists in the town. And she too was concerned about the often cramped home conditions of Polynesian families. She saw it as unfavourable to their children's progress at school. An elderly resident who has helped promote sporting activities in the town for many years feels hostile towards one of the main football clubs because member-ship has become almost completely European. He regarded the other main club as providing 'more enjoyment' as there were 'Maoris, Islanders, and Whites, and no discrimination'. A young mother, who had apparently had more favourable experiences, believed that the 'different races' in Tokoroa 'got along pretty well'. She had recently gone to a party where 'just about every race was there'. 'There was no scrapping,' she said, and she enjoyed it.

From the ethnographic accounts, too, come several casual references to informal cordial contact between Polynesian and European during the course of the interview. In one case a Samoan woman 'dropped in' on her European neighbour and the observer noted that 'they were obviously the best of friends'. One unusual and poignant case involved an elderly widower (European) and a woman neighbour (Maori). After the funeral of the man's wife, several years previously, an 11-year-old Maori boy appeared at his door and said that his mother told him to come and stay with the old man to keep him company. The man could now say, 'the boy has been a great help, and stays most of the time in my house'.

We have examined each major ethnic, cultural, and national group, noting especially those characteristics which are likely to have influenced the kind of adaptation or adjustment that adult members of each experience in the new town environment. And we have surveyed a range of attitudes and sentiments, mainly from the European side. The argument for treating two categories, European and Polynesian, as the major ones in trying to understand this process would seem to have been sustained, although with some justification for regarding the Samoan group as being atypical in some important respects. Our task now is to develop more generally applicable insights based upon these particular ones, and to obtain an 'overview' of pattern and process as it affects and is affected by these many kinds of people.

It has been truly stated that 'questions of status are the heart of racial and ethnic relations; these relations, indeed, can scarcely be said to exist if there is no question of status', and that 'a good deal of each person's inner drama is discovery of the identity given him by others and his reactions to it and the people who define him so' (Hughes and Hughes 1952: 101–102).

It is a harsh fact that Maori and other Polynesian people enjoy less than their proportionate share of public or wider community status, a status which is based largely upon a combination of occupation and income. These people are likely to be semi skilled mill workers, bushworkers, or unskilled labourers; less likely to be tradesmen or clerks; far less likely to be businessmen (however 'small'), teachers, or other professionals. They are more likely to have community prestige in the field of sport and entertainment (see Chapter 4), but the rewards for this are less tangible than those based upon occupation. They are not so easily convertible into forms of material security such as a loan to purchase a more spacious and comfortable home or the means to obtain a 'superior' education for one's children. Such inequality is linked to the cultural differences we started with; the relative unfamiliarity of Polynesian peoples with European commercial enterprise and techniques for 'getting on' in the world. And they are perhaps less motivated to do so, especially if this means failing to meet the expectations of kinsmen. Their level of formal educational attainment is usually lower, and raising it is generally regarded by the people themselves as the beginning of the way out of their status dilemma—for their children rather than for themselves.

Status is reflected in housing: the largest and most convenient homes belong to Europeans (who have the smallest families); the smallest and least convenient dwellings carry the greatest proportion of Polynesian families. It is true that there is a broad category of more spacious and convenient company houses, including homes being purchased by employees, in which Polynesian people are more fairly represented. But the fact that the extremes exist is disturbing.

A front page headline news item in the South Waikato News for 13 June 1972, contains the following statements:

Unemployment and Accomodation are Problems for Maori and Islander.
Unemployment of unskilled workers and lack of temporary accommodation were the two main problems facing Maoris and Islanders in Tokoroa, according to the newly appointed Maori and Island Affairs Department Officer, Mr J. Papali ... He estimated that as many as 200 people were unemployed in the Tokoroa area... 'Jobs for unskilled workers are particularly scarce in the Tokoroa area at the moment' he said.

As long as there is full employment and the opportunity for 'overtime' work the Polynesian sector of the workforce will not be unduly prejudiced, even if incomes reveal some sharp racial inequalities at the extremes. But any security which rests upon this situation is precarious for those with least bargaining power.

We must add to this vulnerability based upon occupational class a prior set of handicaps (not forgetting all the while that Polynesian people are visible as such). This takes us back to the most basic cultural differences: of ancestral languages and the values they embody; of the strength of kinship bonds and sentiment. And it includes the history of economic and political subordination of Polynesian to European. Prosperous or poor, a Polynesian person is likely to suffer a lack of confidence in the face of European forms of social organization (formal or informal) and European language and custom generally. As a member of a minority culture a Polynesian person is more likely to be exposed to feelings of whakamaa—a compound of shame, shyness, and lack of confidence. Mrs A.R. was referring to this at the end of her testimony (see page 42). Mr L.P., a Cook Island elder, felt it also —in spite of his long association with Europeans in Tokoroa and a fair command of English—when he started his speech with the words 'I will try to come out of my hiding place'. He later stated the case quite plainly for his people:

Concerning the mixing of the Island people with the rest of the
community, you will find that the Cook Islanders are shy in
many respects, and that is why they do not mix very well with
the people here. As far as willingness . . . to participate in
anything, I would say that there is no more willing race than
they. . . . However, it is shyness that stops them. There is also
the fact that we are strangers in this country and we come to
meetings like this because we are invited; we will only come as
guests; we will not push our way in.

Europeans who cannot understand why so many Maori and
Polynesian people prefer the company of their familiars simply
fail to recognize the crucial importance of this task of 'protecting
the self', and how it is even more important for a 'visible' member
of a minority culture which in its traditional form was until recently a whole world away from that of the dominant culture. In
the face of criticism, from Europeans mainly, this task is part of
the 'inner drama' being enacted amongst many hundreds of
people in the town of Tokoroa.

When in the next chapters we survey the expanding ground of
common interest and common enterprise in this town, we may be
encouraged to think that the dilemma described above may not
continue indefinitely. Meanwhile, in any new town situation[7] the
most immediately meaningful task for any person, European or
Polynesian, is to find relief and relaxation from the exacting
tasks of earning a livelihood and raising a family and to acquire
some measure of felt personal worth and status no matter how
limited and locally defined this worth and status might be.
Hence the importance of primary or face-to-face group situations
which offer an opportunity for the expression of one's emotions or
interests and the opportunity to be recognized for what one is
worth. The family household offers the most common day to day
opportunities for expression and recognition, at least ideally.
It is often supplemented by networks and cliques of neighbourhood friends and sometimes by clubs and associations of various
kinds. Maori and other Polynesian people are not unique in these
respects. But outside of family, kin, and close friends we may see
how and why these people tend to tread more warily, with less
time, inclination, or appropriate knowledge to penetrate far
into the European world of commerce, politics, or its own brands

of minor social and cultural sophistication, though some do.

The churches in Tokoroa must be credited with some attempt to address themselves to problems associated with migration and the need for social and cultural adjustment. Their contribution would seem to be of a twofold, complementary nature. The 'ethnic' churches provide salutary cultural 'islands', in time and space. Thus the Pacific Island Presbyterian (Congregational) Church is well attended by Samoan, Cook Island, and Niuean peoples. Regular services are offered in the various vernacular languages. It is a church for young and old, and a wide variety of sporting, social, and cultural activities are organised around the basis of church membership. To a lesser extent, other denominations offer similar ethnic fellowship. The Methodist Church with its Maori Mission, both the Seventh Day Adventist and the Church of Latter Day Saints (Mormon) with their appeal to Maori and other Polynesian peoples, and, of course, the Roman Catholic Church.

Interdenominational co-operation, including joint enterprise directed towards problems of cultural adjustment and the maintenance of good will among ethnic groups, is almost certainly an under-developed field in Tokoroa. But, there are encouraging signs. The Ministers' Fraternal, which in 1972 was led by a Methodist (Maori) and an Anglican (Pakeha) is concerned with improving communication across denominational and ethnic boundaries. Such conscious interdominational effort has already led to a series of fruitful home study evenings at which church members of several denominations and cultures (including various Polynesian ones) met to discuss the special problems faced by Pacific Island settlers in Tokoroa. Because active, serious participation in church affairs is generally low amongst most sections of the townspeople (see Chapter 4) one cannot claim too much community effect from such efforts. But the mere fact that they exist is encouraging, and it exemplifies the second of the complementary approaches employed by at least some of the churches and church adherents in the town.

As a major denomination the Roman Catholic Church is worth special note. In its organisation and auxiliary activities the Catholic Church in Tokoroa expresses both complementary approaches; it recognizes and respects the special needs of ethnic groups—

especially those of Maori and Pacific Island peoples—and, it also pursues the ideal of free and fruitful communication between and among all ethnic groups. One occasion of active concern originating from the Catholic congregation provides us with a felicitous note on which to close this chapter. The item quoted appeared in the South Waikato News, 11 November 1971.

About 280 people representing various ethnic groups in Tokoroa, gathered together for an international dinner and social at the Catholic Hall last Saturday.
Apart from New Zealanders, others to attend the function were Samoans, Dutch, English, Maori and Cook Islanders. The Evening was organised by the Catholic Inter-Racial Committee ... The Organisers described the occasion as a big success in that it achieved its purpose of promoting better understanding between the various ethnic groups.

NOTES

1 These concepts, which are defined briefly in *Report of the Secretary for Maori Affairs*, 1960 (the 'Hunn Report'), page 15, will be applied towards the end of this chapter. It is enough to note now that 'assimilation' implies the eventual loss of all unique cultural characteristics by the person or group that is 'assimilating' to the other culture. 'Integration' does not, or ought not to, imply necessary loss of original or unique identity by the 'integrating' or closely co-operating groups.

2 Numbers and proportions of the various ethnic groups are very difficult to ascertain. The Maori figures (for Tokoroa: 15 per cent for 1966; 17 per cent for 1971) can be obtained from official censuses but are based upon the criterion of ancestry, not felt identity which is a more sociologically justifiable criterion. The university survey (see Swain 1970) made finer distinctions based upon islands of origin or felt identify but the effective sample is statistically suspect for Polynesian groups. In this chapter I use a combination of census, survey, and Department of Maori and Island Affairs estimates and make no apology for the resulting 'round figures'.

3 The Caledonian Associations, represented in Tokoroa by a highland pipe band, seem to be a New Zealand institution and almost as old as European settlement in this country.

4 A series of four evening 'workshops' was held at the Tokoroa High School during May 1970. They were organized and conducted jointly by Father Ray Selby on behalf of the Tokoroa Survey Committee and the author on behalf of the University of Waikato. The average attendance was about 50 per night. Approximately 6 people of Polynesian ancestry attended over the whole course. See later chapters for further reference to 'workshop' events and findings.

5 See Pitt and Macpherson, *Emerging Pluralism*, for a full discussion of the nature and function of the Samoan 'āiga or extended family.

6 This is supported by a statement from the Tokoroa District Probation Officer (see *South Waikato News*, 3 February 1972), and refers to cases handled by his office. Less than 1 per cent of these were 'Pacific Islanders'; approximately 80 per cent were 'of Maori extraction'. I would take the 'Pacific Islanders' to mean primarily Samoans.

7 The 'new town situation' is emphasized by the university survey figures for length of residence (in 1969): 86 per cent of the households had lived in Tokoroa for 10 years or less; 60 per cent for only 5 years or less; and 1 in every 6 had lived in the town for less than 1 year. The implications of these figures for the task of establishing and maintaining oneself, socially, in this town are, in my opinion, profound.

Shaping a Community 4

The growth and pattern of voluntary association and club life.
The range and extent of participation. The emphasis upon sport
and recreation. Church membership and church activity.

... the neighbours all follow different pursuits as far as social
life is concerned. Mr and Mrs Klomp and Mr Hoslefoot are
card-playing fans, Mr and Mrs Mason are much involved in
Scouting, the Hadles badminton, Mr and Mrs Slatford tennis
and writing reports for the Country Session on the radio, Miss
Hoslefoot basketball and Scouting, Mrs Doofield an artist and
her husband Art Society, and Mr and Mrs Newfield and son
George are involved in horse riding competitions ...

excerpt from a neighbourhood study

Well known and respected business man and a former
Chairman of the Tokoroa County Town Committee, Mr H.J.
Spear left a wide gap in these ranks when he collapsed and died
on January 22.

Mr Spear's interests included the Y.M.C.A., the formation
of the Pipe Band, promoting the swimming baths, promoting
county subdivisions in Tokoroa, acting as a riding member of
of the Matamata County Council, being a member of the St
Francis vestry, the Tokoroa Rotary Club and the Masonic
Lodge.

South Waikato News 1969

One of the most ancient drives behind local group decision-
making and local community action has been the need for people
who share a common space with common or overlapping problems to work together upon their environment to shape and
control it. For people in new industrial towns and settlements this
need and force still operates, although it is increasingly compli-

cated and sometimes obstructed or displaced by social forces operating in and from the society at large.

Within the local industrial organization itself (notably, the mill) there is generated a 'community' of work. There are crosscutting sets of face-to-face relationships, common understandings within and between these sets, and kinds and degrees of identification with the organization as a whole or with one of its subsystems (including trade union organizations). But what of the residential community?

Houses and certain basic services are first supplied by the industrial organization, the company, with the help of specialized agencies (Ministry of Works, County Councils, Education Boards). These are seldom complete in their range; seldom adequate to meet the rapidly expanding needs of a new community. Moreover, they have taken shape, characteristically, from slide-rule and drawing board, with one eye always on the balance sheet. The planners' conception, even where it materializes in a generous financial climate, is never likely to be the complete answer to people's needs; not even their needs of today and certainly not their needs of tomorrow. Even the siting of timber towns has produced a range of unfulfilled needs or unforeseen problems for the inhabitants. The general area is determined by the physical requirements of the industry and the actual site by engineering facility (for roading, drainage, water and power supply, etc.), and the cost of title and development. Some important human factors are often neglected.

Thus Tokoroa was founded upon a more or less flat, fairly exposed site, on company land 6 kilometres from the industrial plant, straddling a main arterial highway. (These last two facts in themselves are creating problems; the town has spread too close to the mill with its smoke and fumes, and the now very busy highway has tended to isolate the smaller eastern residential area.) It is only 20 minutes easy travelling from the nearest established town, Putaruru, but an hour or more by road from the nearest cities of Hamilton and Rotorua. A more congenial but much more expensive site for the town might have been at Mangakino—39 kilometres away on the Waikato River—where a city of considerable character and charm could have been developed. Or at Putaruru where the resources of two kinds of community and economy—dairying and timber—might have combined to produce a new urban community of even greater variety and wealth, besides being somewhat closer (at least 'psychologically' closer) to the older established and more sophisticated centres of Hamilton and Rotorua. As it is, Tokoroa must build up its character and a congenial physical environment the hard way—for example, the creation of a large artificial lake for recreation is currently being planned for the town. Meanwhile, thousands of residents escape by motor car each week; some no doubt to more stimulating or pleasant environments.[1]

The relative isolation of Tokoroa seems to have contributed also to the very slow development of secondary manufacturing industries in the town; certainly there is no shortage of trainable labour for a wide range of light manufactures. It is likely also that the unfortunate choice of site might be among the reasons why so few people expect to retire in the town—less than 1 in 5, according to the 1969 university survey.

Within the town, too, there has been a failure to make far-sighted investments in human welfare and this is demonstrated first in housing layout and house design. Residential planning has tended to compound the errors common to most new subdivisions in New Zealand towns and cities. On the other hand, actual house design and quality seems to be improving. This certainly appears to be true for the newer company houses being built for letting and for purchase by employees, but earlier company houses were not particularly well designed or appointed for a working man—often a shift-worker—with a young and some-times large family. (Residential layout and housing will be examined in more detail in Chapter 6.) Such physical environ-mental shortcomings have social repercussions. They draw various responses from the residents, some of which become the stuff of action at neighbourhood level, while others are articulated through various voluntary associations, and some through local political action (see Chapters 7 and 8).

Similar conclusions can be drawn if we examine the provisions made for essential services in, say, education and health. The state is usually diligent, at least initially, in supplying primary and even secondary educational services. However, demand exceeds supply from time to time. In Tokoroa, both professional teaching organizations and parent-teacher bodies have been exerting strenuous pressure upon the regional and national education authorities to expedite school building programmes and to address themselves to equally urgent problems of teacher shortage and teacher-pupil ratios. In 1960 local submissions were made to a commission of inquiry into education, making a plea for the special educational needs of Tokoroa and claiming that children's education was suffering. Ten years later, parent-teacher and professional teaching organisations were still putting pressure upon regional and state educational bodies to provide more schools, more and better classrooms, and more teachers.

Pre-school services are often woefully inadequate in rapidly expanding communities of young families. Until 1971 Tokoroa had only 2 kindergartens (with a total waiting list of over 500) and 1 playcentre for an estimated pre-school population of 3000. However, local groups were co-operating to help expand these services; a new kindergarten was opened in August 1971 after a 3 year effort, and another was being planned. In addition, the Roman Catholic Church has provided for pre-school needs among its Maori and other Polynesian members by promoting educational play groups which are conducted by the mothers themselves.

Medical services, before a town is large enough to qualify for a general hospital, are undertaken by a handful of overworked general practitioners and state-employed visiting nurses and the St John Ambulance Association. Tokoroa gained its small general hospital in the spring of 1970 after nearly 6 years of lobbying by locals, at regional hospital board and at national departmental level.[2] But the struggle to keep medical facilities abreast of demand continues. Periodic shortages of general practitioners and hospital staff (and the provision of accommodation for these) continue to exercise the attentions and efforts of civic service groups, notably the Jaycees.

It has been appreciated too, by small groups of residents, that health services do not end with the provision of doctors and hospitals. For example, a marriage guidance bureau is being operated by local voluntary counsellors. This service started in 1964 under the auspices of the National Marriage Guidance Council. Early in 1965 the first 2 local people went to Wellington for a training course. By 1970 about 24 cases were being handled annually in 50 or 60 interviews, and group discussions, lectures, and 'family education' evenings were also being held. The work is

financially assisted by the Tokoroa Business and Professional
Women's Club and probably by other voluntary groups as well.
More recently, a wider-purpose 'Samaritan' counselling service
has been established by locals. Pressure has also been applied from
organized resident bodies to have governmental welfare services
(notably, for the Maori and other Polynesian groups) head-
quartered in the town, and it seemed that some success was
imminent. These examples must be seen against a background of
rapid growth and expansion of the community from a settlement
of a few hundred people in 1950 to a town of over 16 000 people in
1970.

Women's voluntary organisations, of which there are 10 or so in
Tokoroa (apart from women's sports groups or hobbies clubs
which cater exclusively for women), have tended to combine a
recreation with a community service function. In the words of a
local columnist, women tend to join these clubs and associations
'for the feeling of achievement, helping others, and the companionship'.

We have already noted the early establishment of the Maori
Women's Welfare League. The oldest established women's
group is the Tokoroa branch of the Women's Division of the
Federated Farmers. The W.D.F.F. branch began in 1930 and enjoyed a membership of 100 in its earlier years—when Tokoroa was
still primarily a farming community. Membership had dropped to
below half of this figure by 1970. Although primarily social-
recreational, in fact the W.D.F.F. still retains a community
service function such as offering a housekeeping service for
ill or hardpressed mothers. Membership is almost entirely
European (Pakeha), unlike the Catholic Women's League which
has about 50 members, representing Polynesian and European
sections of the community and which appears to have been
growing steadily in membership. The Catholic League is involved
not only in fund raising and charities for overseas missions but
also in a wide range of local community affairs. It co-ordinates its
activities with recreational and service groups such as the Intellectually Handicapped Children's Society, Crippled Children's
Society, and the Red Cross.

Two women's groups which in 1970 were struggling to maintain their membership were the Townswomen's Guild and the
Country Girls' Club, although like the others they combine

service with a social recreational function. The Country Girls'
Club received encouragement after organizing Tokoroa's first
rodeo in December 1970—a success which drew some 3 000
people. But the Townswomen's Guild actually went into recess
only 3 years after it was established. An office holder remarked,
'We need 15 members who would attend regularly and be active'.

The most flourishing women's group in the town in 1970–71
was the 'Calorie Counters'. After only a year they had a membership of 70 and Maori women were well represented. The fact that
it was a social-recreational rather than a mixed recreational and
community service group would seem to be symptomatic of the
general predisposition of Tokoroa's adult joiners—who are 3 out
of 4 of the population.

The most impressive collective response of residents to their
environment in a timber town is the formation of sport and recreational clubs. Tokoroa was still a tiny frontier settlement when
it established its Rugby Football Club. In the early days of an industrial community, the residents usually form a general social
club or hall committee which sponsors a range of recreational
activities. But sooner or later an expanding range of clubs and
other cultural groups establish themselves in their own right, with
or without assistance from or affiliation with parent organizations.
The proliferation of sports groups tends to follow a national pattern starting with several standard outdoor and indoor sports such
as rugby football, cricket, hockey, golf, outdoor and indoor
basketball, table tennis, indoor bowls, etc. Tokoroa appears to
have followed this pattern and now all these sports are well represented and many more besides, including such sophisticated
sports groups as the alpine, judo, canoeing and caving clubs
established over the last year or so.

An important feature and function of this remarkable proliferation of clubs would seem to be the quality of performance
measured by national and even world standards. There is no
shortage of sporting idols on the local scene. Kahu Mahanga probably tops the list as every boy's hero; he is a middleweight
boxing champion of Australasian renown and was voted Tokoroa's
'Sportsman of the Year' in 1971. Elliot Kereopa would run a close
second as the Rugby League football star selected to play for New
Zealand in the World Cup Series. Dave Lamberton, who holds
New Zealand and world records for various types of woodchop-

ping events, is a household name. Ted McDougall is a New Zealand champion amateur golfer who has also participated in World Cup events in Europe. Val and John Robinson (husband and wife) are long distance runners of international standing; Val represented New Zealand at the 1970 Commonwealth Games in Edinburgh. Carolyn Gardiner was New Zealand 'Roller Skating Queen' in 1970. These are only a few of the prominent sportsmen and sportswomen whose names, faces, and performances were, or are, continually in the public eye, and who bring pride and renown to the 'sportsminded' community.

'Name another town the size of Tokoroa, or even twice as large, that can produce sportsmen of such high calibre, you just could not,' said the guest speaker, an ex-New Zealand cricket captain, at the 1971 'Sportsman of the Year' function. He finished his statement amidst loud applause.

There are well over 50 sports clubs in Tokoroa now, with membership varying from several hundred (in the major sports, like Rugby and Rugby League), to a couple of dozen in the more unusual groups. According to the 1969 survey (of 'individuals') in Tokoroa, sports clubs lead the field in popularity with nearly 15 per cent of the sample claiming membership solely or preponderantly in such groups. (See Table 3; 'hobbies' are included in this figure, but membership size in these clubs is usually small). Even the two next most popular categories—'leadership' and 'workers clubs', with 10.6 and 11 per cent respectively—include a fair measure of at least indoor sports among their activities.

As a class, sports clubs would seem to be the most eclectic of all voluntary associations in their recruitment of members from a wide range of ethnic and occupational categories. Certainly, in the timber town, they provide significant social links which cut across these divisions and also the spatial ones of neighbourhood and district. Convivial social events, sometimes organized and semi-formal but often spontaneous and quite informal, accompany most sporting activities. Friendships and even marriages may spring from these common experiences. The significance of sports clubs in creating a new social fabric in these towns should not be underestimated. To a lesser extent, the other cultural interest groups—the hobbies and fine-arts groups for example—also serve this function.

Somewhat less eclectic, by definition, are the ethnic cultural groups, (Table 3, class 5). But the community building function of most of these groups would also seem to be considerable—if in a less direct and obvious way. A 'synthetic' community such as a timber town is not like the village and small town communities of history; it cannot offer a homogeneous world view and a common experience to each of its members over a wide range of thought and activity. The synthetic community draws its members from a bewildering variety of cultural milieux. Most come as adults, faced with the immediate and urgent task of making a minimal social adjustment to this new and (for some) very strange environment. This can be an exacting and socially hazardous task for anyone, but more especially for those people who are least familiar with the language and customs of the dominant culture. The ethnic voluntary associations provide social islands to which their members may retreat periodically, and bases out of which they may operate to do necessary business with the less familiar and sometimes less accepting social world around them. These may be seen as principle functions of the several ethnic associations and especially those of the Maori and Pacific Island residents. Some of these are associated with churches. Some, like the Maori Women's Welfare League, are affiliated to an important national organization which performs excellent and necessary welfare functions in collaboration with other agencies.

The Pacific Island peoples are the most prominent in their formation of ethnic clubs—even in sporting activities. But this is not to say that in their activities they do not meet peoples of other ethnic groups, Maori and European. Even in the following example of a special Cook Islander event, there was occasion for a variety of communication and exchange, both formal and informal. At Labour Week-end 1971, local Cook Islander sports teams played Auckland Cook Islander teams at Tokoroa. Arrangements were made to use the High School sports fields. The Mayor of Tokoroa welcomed the visiting teams and their supporters and the general public was welcome to watch the events. There was a dance on the Saturday night in the Catholic Hall and a church service at the Pacific Island Congregational Church on the Sunday. The Operatic Hall was booked for a 'midnight dance' on Sunday night and there was a tennis tournament on the following day at the High School courts. At various levels and stages there was co-operation and co-ordination between the Cook Island people and other groups and individuals in the community.

Finally, in this brief review of voluntary associations, there are the civic service groups. In Table 1 these include 2 broad types. Organizations such as Civil Defence, St John Ambulance, and the Volunteer Fire Brigade, by the more immediately practical nature of their tasks appear to recruit a more varied class and ethnic membership than the 'service' organizations—the Jaycees, Chamber of Commerce, Lions, Rotary and Rotoract. The latter type tends to attract, if not favour, membership from the business and professional sections of the community. Together, all these associations are not well represented in membership numbers (not quite 6 per cent of the sample). Together they stand for kinds of activity which are conceptually distinct from those of sporting and most other recreational and cultural groups.[3] Generally, the interests and activities of the civic service groups are directed either wholly towards the needs of the total community or these form an important part of the avowed interests and objectives of the organization. The actual interest and activity might be specific, as in the St John Ambulance and Fire Brigade groups, or diffuse and require continuous definition as in the 'projects' of Jaycees, or Lions. (The service groups and their work will be discussed more fully in Chapter 8.)

A caricature of Tokoroa residents would depict them as far too busy working overtime, chasing balls of all shapes and sizes, or motoring out of town to lakes and beaches, to ever give serious thought to questions of community welfare and town government. This would appear to contain some truth but is not a particularly just or helpful diagnosis.

Tokoroa residents have created an impressive array of voluntary organizations in which special interest groups predominate. The 1970 Tokoroa handbook *Inquire Within* (compiled and published by the Jaycees) lists these (see Table 1).

To this we could add 11 churches, (see below p 71) each with auxiliary groups, not all of which are included in the list. One point to note is the large number of welfare groups. If to these we add civic service groups and others, like the Maori service groups mentioned, the Business and Professional Women's group, the Kindergarten and Play Centre Associations and the dozen school

TABLE 1
TOKOROA VOLUNTARY ORGANIZATIONS

		Number
Agricultural (e.g. Federated Farmers, A. & P., Young Farmers)		5
Civic (e.g. Jaycees, Lions, Orphans Club, Fire Brigade)		8
Gardening Clubs		8
Hobbies and Cultural (incl. Fine Arts Societies)		17
Lodges and Friendly Societies		2
Returned Services (e.g. R.S.A., ex P.O.W., Air Force Association)		6
Sports: Bowls (indoor and outdoor)	6	
Cricket	5	
Rugby and Rugby League	9	
Others	27	
Total	47	47
Welfare (e.g. Birthright, Crippled Children, Red Cross, Marriage Guidance, Senior Citizens, Plunket, and including 7 Scouting and Guide groups)		27
Women's Organizations (e.g. Catholic Women's League, Business and Professional Women, Nurses' Association, Jaycettes, Country Girls' Club)		10
Maori Organizations (e.g. Maori Wardens' Association, M.W.W.L., Catholic Maori Society)		5
Miscellaneous (e.g. Kennel Club, Pony Club, Road Safety Council, Kindergarten Association, Play Centre, Aero Club, Retailers' Association)		13
TOTAL		**148**

committees (also not listed above), we have a large proportion indeed of groups which are oriented towards some aspect or other of community service and welfare. The suggestion that Tokoroa residents are primarily pleasure seeking in their club life may need qualifying. But what about actual joining? To what extent do the residents use their voluntary associations? A favourable comparison emerges when the figures for membership taken from the 1969 survey are placed alongside those of a much longer established but similarly prosperous town of comparable size.[4] (See Table 2.)

A common complaint in most associational life, probably throughout New Zealand, is that people who are willing to join are not always as willing to share the work of organization and administration of their clubs. That this is true for Tokoroa is

suggested by the figure of 84 per cent, for one sample, who said
that they never go to meetings.[5] Occasionally too, there is a
suggestion in the dozens of items of club and sports reporting in
each issue of the local newspaper that people are reluctant to
serve as organizers and administrators. The only illustrations
that come to mind refer to 'parental apathy' in connexion with
kindergarten organisation, the Plunket Society and the Marching

TABLE 2
PROPORTIONS BELONGING TO VOLUNTARY ORGANIZATIONS

	Tokoroa 1969 %	Masterton 1957 %
Belonging to 0	26.0	30.0
Belonging to 1	39.4	34.0
Belonging to 2	16.0	20.0
Belonging to 3	11.0	9.0
Belonging to 4 or more	7.6	7.0

TABLE 3
PATTERNS OF PREFERENCE IN JOINING
Note that this classification is not identical with that of the Jaycee's guide

	%
Outdoor sports clubs and hobbies	14.7
Service organizations (e.g. St Johns, Fire Brigade, Jaycees, Rotary)	5.9
Theatrical, operatic, musical	2.9
'Leadership', including youth organizations, discussion groups	10.6
Committees, including P.T.A., school committees	7.6
(Ethnic) Cultural groups — Samoan, Cook Island, Maori, etc.[a]	4.1
R.S.A., Buffalo Lodge, etc.	8.2
Church organizations	8.8
Workers' Clubs (e.g. Pulp & Paper Workers, Tokoroa Club)	11.2
Not Applicable	26.0
	100.0

[a] As the survey appears to have missed contact with a disproportionate number of
Maori and other Polynesian persons in the original sample, this figure may be too
low.

Association. For example, the president of the Tokoroa Marching Association declared in June 1971 that the club did not have a very active year mainly because of 'the lack of instructors and to the presence of parental apathy'. But although particular groups might face crises from time to time, there is no indication that associational life generally is in danger of waning in Tokoroa as a result of such reluctance.

The picture that emerges is one of the average adult Tokoroa resident as a joiner of at least one club or association but probably not an organiser or committee member. The extent to which the joiner is impelled, primarily, towards recreation and amusement, or towards some specific or general community service remains less clearly discernible—partly because of the classification of data but also because many groups have multiple (recreation and service) functions. The tendency would appear, however, to be towards recreation.

Diffuse religion sentiment is still given public expression, in Tokoroa as in other New Zealand towns and cities. The drama and aesthetics of a religious world-view are probably the most pervasive and enduring, but it is church membership attendance, and church-based social activity which merits special attention here. While from Monday to Saturday—and even on Sunday—the great majority of New Zealand citizens appear to be thoroughly secular, organised religious activity is by no means defunct. Certainly not in Tokoroa, as this item from the *South Waikato News* indicates:

Work has begun on the ($115 000) Pacific Island Congregational Church. [More correctly, 'The Pacific Island Presbyterian Church'. The older and more familiar name, 'Congregational', persists.] $70 000 has so far been raised by special offerings, socials, dances and stage shows (in Tokoroa and in Auckland and the Hawkes Bay). According to their pastor it is and will be 'a firm indication of confidence the Pacific Island people have in the future of Tokoroa'.

There was no need for the pastor to state the obvious, namely that the efforts of his congregation were also a firm indication of confidence in their own religious institution. Admittedly, the

Pacific Island Presbyterians present a shining example to all church adherents in the town, but so do many Roman Catholics and the members of the smaller, less orthodox denominations (most of which attract disproportionately large numbers of non-European members). Individual personal commitment (no matter how weak or faltering) to some faith or other, and to its institutional expression (a church) is still statistically significant.

The figures for 'religious profession' are not indicators of this commitment. Thus, when 35 per cent of one sample in the University survey declared themselves 'Anglican', 18 per cent 'Presbyterian', 16 per cent 'Roman Catholic', 5 per cent 'Methodist', and 2 per cent 'Congregational', the majority of these respondents, especially those in the 2 largest categories, would be stating nominal identity rather than active membership. Disregarding for the moment churches and sects with very small statistical representation, we have already accounted for a good 75 per cent of the adult population (Pitt and Swain 1970: 9). Survey inquiry into church attendance, however, reveals the wide discrepancy between religious 'profession' and religious practice. About 1 person in 5 (18.3 per cent) claimed regular weekly attendance at church; 1 in 8 or 9 (11.6 per cent) attended more than once a quarter; 1 in 12 (8.1 per cent) 4 times a year or less; 1 in 10 (9.5 per cent) attended church at Christmas, Easter, and for rites of passage (funerals, weddings, christenings); nearly a third (32.8 per cent) attended only for rites of passage. The author's comment is interesting:

Overall, the figures suggest that as presently organised and supported, the churches seem unlikely to provide a major focus for involvement in the community, although it could be argued that they possess some potential in this respect.

(Pitt and Swain 1970: 50)

This, at first glance, appears to be a reasonable conclusion, but one could just as easily quote the figures to support an opposite opinion. If the survey figure of 18.3 per cent who 'attended regularly once a week or more frequently' is even moderately reliable, then, as the author himself admits (on the same page) this is 'a not insubstantial minority'. The University's survey of households reveals a supporting figure—24.7 per cent who 'attended church as a family' (Pitt and Swain 1970: 49), while further support comes from a question asked of secondary school pupils in the survey of youth opinion. When asked who should be responsible for organising youth activities in Tokoroa, 23.6 per cent of the respondents named 'the church', a choice which was second only to 'young people themselves' (31 per cent) and more than twice the magnitude of the next most popular choices —'interested adults' and, 'service or community organis-ations' (Pitt 1970: 13). Finally, if the reader refers back to Table 3 (p. 68) on 'patterns of preference in joining' it will be seen that 'church organizations' hold their own fairly well against all other categories except 'outdoor sports clubs and hobbies'. If it is conceded that church attendance is itself a community activity— as much as, say, participation in a sport—then I would suggest that churches and church-based organizations are still among the major focii for community involvement in Tokoroa. To claim more for the churches would not be realistic; to claim less would not be fair.

Ten denominations and 11 churches are officially represented in the town. All or most of these have one or several auxiliary organizations. Omitting Sunday schools and Bible classes these include:

Pacific Island Presbyterian	Boys's Brigade; Girl Guides; Brownies; Youth Club; Ladies' Meeting.
Roman Catholic	Catholic Women's League; Catholic Youth Group; Scout Troops; Catholic Maori Group.
Church of England	Anglican Guide; Friendly Circle; Young Wives' Groups.
Latter Day Saints (Mormon)	Mutual Improvement Association; Relief Society.
Methodist	Woman's Fellowship; Scout Troops and Club packs.

Presbyterian	Women's Fellowship.
Seventh Day Adventist	Health and Welfare Society; Pathfinders' Club.
Salvation Army	Women's Home League
Open Brethren	Women's Fellowship; Boys' and Girls' Rallies; Teen Time.
Baptist	Junior, Intermediate, Senior, and Pioneer Brigades; Youth Fellowship; Ladies' Friendly Circle; Women's Missionary Union.
Reformed Church	Women's Fellowship.

Both the Methodist and the Anglican Churches employ special Maori pastors, and since 1971 the Anglican church has also employed an experienced, full-time male social worker. Other aspects of the social role of churches and their auxiliary organizations have been discussed in Chapter 3. Narrow sectarianism with crude and simplistic belief and sentiment still exist, but the trend amongst most churches and their congregations appears to be towards more secular and social concern. If the trend continues, and if interdenominational liaison is maintained and enlarged, there would seem to be no doubt about the continuing contribution which churches will make to the main stream of social and cultural life in the community. The churches in Tokoroa also have the great asset of relatively youthful congregations, and a teen-aged generation that does not regard the religious institutions and beliefs of their parent generation as a source of misunderstanding between them (see Pitt 1970: 20).

Church, by definition, is fellowship, and fellowship is a major attribute of community. Even were we to disregard the special spiritual commission of the church we would still have to recognize it as an institution which helps people to live together, to be responsible for one another, and to feel wanted. It thus takes its place beside (and in conjunction with) the family, the neighbourhood, the school, the pub, and the club.

NOTES

1 According to the 1969 university survey (Pitt and Swain 1970: 47) 62 per cent of the households surveyed reported that 'more often than not, they spend ordinary week-ends away from Tokoroa'. It was estimated that in 1970, 85 per cent of the Tokoroa households owned a motor vehicle.

2 A local Hospital Promotions Committee was established for this purpose. The need for a general hospital was more than justified. After just 1 year of service it had received over 2600 patients and treated 1180 outpatients. Nearly 800 operations were performed; more than 2600 x-rays and over 5000 physiotherapy treatments were given.

3 Partial exceptions would be a few ethnic and cultural groups which, like the Rahui Marae Committee and Maori Women's Welfare League, are also concerned with wider community affairs. One should also include groups which pursue specific but less widely acknowledged community services, e.g. The Marriage Guidance Counsellors, the Orphans Club, and Intellectually Handicapped Children's Society. These and several others are active in Tokoroa.

4 Masterton; population 15 400 in 1961, three years after the survey referred to. See Robb and Somerset 1957: 33.

5 Against this figure we must note another seemingly contradictory one. Namely, that one third of all households with school-aged children, i.e. 23 per cent of the sample, claimed that at least one parent attended 'all or most' P.T.A. meetings. (Pitt and Swain 1970: 48–49).

The Young People of 5
Tokoroa

Youth as a 'minority' group. Facilities for education and recreation. Vocational aspirations and prospects. Activities of youth
'Delinquency'. The young as critics and shapers of their
environment.

'Numerically the largest of the minorities and one which is an
integral part of the present town, and the essential part of the
future of the town, are the youth'.

(Pitt 1970: 1)

'Our only crime is that we are young.'

(Brian Burmester, editor, South Waikato News)

'Youth' and 'young people' are very relative terms. In the second
quotation above, the editor is referring to the youthfulness of the
adult population which, in 1970, revealed a mean age of only 37
years compared with the New Zealand average of 45 years. Mr
Burmester elaborated:

People think that because it is a young town it must be faultily
run. In other towns you have to be in the place for 20 years
before you can become secretary of the cricket club. Here we
have to get things done quickly, and so much of what we do is
new. Our mayor, who is 34 years old, goes to meetings of a
council [the Matamata County Council, not the local Borough
Committee] which has had only 4 chairmen in 100 years.[1]

There is, of course, a very close relationship between this
youthfulness of the adult population (given a reasonably balanced
sex ratio), and the numbers and increase rate of the dependent
young. If we define 'youth' and 'young people' somewhat arbitrar-
ily as those under 18 we find that in 1970 these 'young people'

were approximately 56 per cent of the whole population of the town. Why then, does Professor Pitt call this section a 'minority'?

A minority, in the sociological sense, usually refers to a category of persons in a population or society which has less public status—less social, political, or economic power in relation to other categories of persons. Thus, non-Europeans (in our society) are a minority in relation to Europeans; women are a minority in relation to men; children a minority in relation to adults. This *pluralist* way of looking at a society or a community is very useful. It helps us to understand and appreciate more fully the dynamic processes which continually modify and shape our social life. It draws attention to the simple yet profound fact that not even the simplest and most closely-knit human communities are composed of people who all enjoy identical interests and advantages. The *differing* interests and advantages, whether we view these in terms of individual persons, or, sets of persons who share similar interests and advantages (or disadvantages), give rise to various forms of striving and competition, and often social strain and conflict. This is more obvious when we apply the principle to say, Maori-Pakeha relations or worker-management relations. It is not so widely recognised that the principle can be applied also to help us understand more about the position and problems of young people (and of women) in our society. For example, we would no longer regard the current movement by secondary school pupils to form their own unions as bizarre. As in other minority groups in society, the members themselves are not always in the best position to effect improvements to their own condition. In fact, young people have been expressly denied this right until very recently and very young children must of necessity have their rights championed (if not defined) by adults.

Young people are unique as a minority group in that each member is in the process of moving out of his or her minority status and, in so doing, is anticipating and preparing for other kinds of social classification—notably those based upon sex, ethnic background, and occupational class. As young people approach school leaving age their identity is increasingly complicated by these other factors. They are not just young people as distinct from adults but may also be aware of themselves as male as distinct from female, Maori as distinct from Pakeha, and as potential members of one occupational or class category as distinct from another. All this is superimposed upon what is for young people the most crucial task of all, the maintenance of self (self-respect or feeling of worthwhileness' amongst a community of peers, playmates, class mates, and fellow members of cliques or gangs). This is a process which starts early in life, is critically important over the middle years of childhood and in adolescence, and probably never ceases to be important. It is a process which is affected, often profoundly, by the awareness that they are children and thus subject to varying degrees of authority, toleration (or lack of it), and understanding (or misunderstanding) from the adult world.

In Tokoroa, this 'minority' is large (in fact, a numerical majority) and obvious. At certain times of the day, notably between 8 and 9 o'clock in the morning and between 3 and 4 o'clock in the afternoon, they seem to 'take over' the streets as they ply to and from the many schools around town.

The schools are the only major institution which caters specifically for the special needs and interests of this 'largest of minorities' in the town. The houses, neighbourhoods, and streets are not designed for young people although they, rather than adults, are more commonly seen in and around these places. Parks and reserves have been provided, for organised recreation mainly, but the small children of many neighbourhoods have no quick or safe access to these and must confine most of their activities to the home section or to the street. Relatively few of the many clubs and associations are established primarily for young people (that is, children and teenagers, as the term is used here). Although ubiquitous, they nevertheless tend to be a neglected section of the population (along with their mothers, some would say); neglected by the architects, planners, and administrators of the town and its life. At least, that is one side of the picture.

This partial neglect begins to show early in the life of a child. Children are born into the town at the rate of about 50 each month or about 600 each year.[2] In 1970 it was necessary for the local maternity unit to transfer almost a third of its admissions to the maternity ward at Hamilton Public Hospital, 97 kilometres away. Admittedly, it is the parents and especially the mothers who feel the direct effects of this paucity of services at this stage in the child's life, but the effects may well be visited upon the child sooner or later. In early infancy it is both mother and child who suffer the effects of neighbourhoods ill-designed for the freedom of small children (for examples of this see Chapter 6). Later in infancy both again suffer from the paucity of pre-school services (see above page 61). Maori and Polynesian children in particular have tended to miss out on pre-school facilities.

Kindergarten teachers in Tokoroa are concerned about the small number of Polynesian children attending kindergarten in the town. Because of this they have arranged a Polynesian parents and childrens afternoon.

South Waikato News, 26 February 1970

Early in 1971 a Catholic Maori pre-school group started in the Church Hall. Twenty-three children (only a tiny fraction of an estimated 1000 pre-school children of Maori and Polynesian parentage) were soon attending the bi-weekly sessions. A Pacific Islander group was also established at the Catholic Hall and later these groups received some encouragement and support from the Play Centre Association and local Play Centre personnel. Some of the women even trained for their 'mother helper' and supervisor's certificates under a programme administered by the Play Centres Association. Later that year several specialists in Maori pre-school education from the Department of Education visited Tokoroa to encourage and stimulate this venture by Maori and Pacific Islander mothers.

The importance of this trend cannot be overestimated, for most of the schools in Tokoroa have a large numerical minority of Maori and other Polynesian children on their rolls. It is commonly recognized that these children (as a class, although there are many exceptions) have greater difficulty with the English language, make slower progress than their European peers, and, at secondary school level, drop out earlier and with much lower academic qualifications. There is thus a severe restriction of choice for these young adults when they seek vocational opportunities; they are much more likely to have to accept work which offers little intrinsic interest and intellectual challenge, low public status, and perhaps even low pay.

A woman school teacher retiring in 1971 after 20 years at a Tokoroa primary school said she was encouraged by 'the upsurge in parent participation among both Maoris and Islanders' in the affairs of that school. If this, and the pre-school movement amongst Catholic Maori and other Polynesian mothers, are true indications of a more general 'upsurge' of interest and participation by the parents of these children, then there is hope that the current cycle of educational under-achievement leading to lower economic status in adults with its effects visited back upon their children, may be modified for Maori and Pacific Island sections of the population.[3]

There were (in 1972) 8 primary schools and 1 intermediate school in Tokoroa.

TABLE 4
APPROXIMATE SCHOOL ROLLS IN 1972

School	Number
Amisfield	160
David Henry	340
Tokoroa Central	450
Tokoroa North	560
Tokoroa Intermediate	900
Tokoroa East	335
Matarawa	400
Strathmore	535
Balmoral	670
TOTAL CHILDREN	**4350**

At the same time, there was 1 high school with a roll of over 1200. A second high school was opened in 1974, and at the beginning of 1975 the combined high school roll was slightly over 1600. Crises arise from time to time, due to shortages of classroom space, recreational facilities, and (to a lesser extent) teaching staff. Common class size seems to approach 40 whereas fewer than 30 children is recommended for schools which have a high proportion of non-European children. (About one third of the children in Tokoroa primary schools are of Maori or other Polynesian ancestry, although this ratio drops to only about 1 in 4 in the high school). Headteachers, parent-teacher bodies, and representatives of the 2 major teacher associations (primary and secondary) publicize these ever expanding needs and lobby for improvements.

The primary school experience extends over a period of 6 to 8 years of each child's life, It is no doubt the greatest single factor (though many-sided and complex in itself) in securing cohesion or working consensus for tomorrow's urban society. All primary school children enjoy a maximum of exposure to approximately the same kinds of adult influence and authority, approximately the same informal social milieux in the classroom and playground, and use approximately the same mode of communication for approximately the same purposes. Children of whatever cultural or class background are thus engaged, for 6 or 7 hours each day, in the task of developing common understandings and skills with their peers. This cannot be matched in scale and comprehensiveness by the family, the neighbourhood, the various clubs which attract children outside of school hours, or the high school, which begins to sort out children more rigorously according to destined adult roles, a process which, we must never forget, starts less obtrusively in the primary schools.

At the beginning of each year some 400 children enter the high school as new pupils—a figure which is growing steadily. The original high school is modern, well equipped, usually fully staffed (although not always entirely with 'qualified' teachers), and its principal could be regarded as progressive by current standards. The school's main problem has been overcrowding, with heavy demands upon space and equipment since at least 1969. The school enjoys fair pass rates in the public examinations.[4] Recreational and club life is well developed. Student 'democracy' of the kind which has evolved over the past ten years in many schools in New Zealand, is also established in this high school and the prefect system was abolished in 1970. All sixth and seventh form students share responsibilities on a roster system. A student council of 20 is elected on a form-level basis, to deal with all domestic matters concerning pupils and relations between pupils and staff. The spirit and direction which the principal seems to be fostering in the school is perhaps indicated also by the choice of guest speakers at the 1971 senior school prizegiving. Instead of the principal himself delivering the usual moral exhortation, or arranging for the most prominent available member of 'the establishment' to do it for him, the guests were Graham Dingle and

Jill Tremain, the young couple who had recently made their
epic journey together along the entire length of the Southern
Alps. The speakers' theme was 'Do your own thing' regardless
of the stultifying pressures of school and society—a very progressive message indeed!

All this is not to claim that Tokoroa's teenage school pupils
enjoy an educational Elysium. Shades of Victorian authority
still haunt even the most progressive of our secondary schools. The
anxiety of the public examination system hangs over all. And much
of what we teach must seem arbitrary or irrelevant to many of
today's young people. The survey on 'Youth Opinion' (Pitt 1970)
suggests areas of concern amongst pupils from the fourth form
upwards. First choices on the importance of 'school issues' elicited
only 3 outstanding emphases in a list of twelve. (See Table 5.)

The high school, for many young people, is their last formal
educational experience. And of the 276 school leavers in 1969,

TABLE 5
OPINIONS ON SCHOOL ISSUES [a]
(Proportions of first choices)

Field of Opinion	Boys %	Girls %
Student democracy	29.7	22.2
Abolition of caning and strapping	6.8	1.4
Abolition of the compulsory wearing of school uniforms	4.1	1.4
Shortage of qualified teachers	18.9	27.8
A need for specially trained student counsellors	1.4	4.2
A need for a national union of secondary school students	1.4	2.8
A need for well conducted courses on sex and family education	4.1	4.2
Abolition of school certificate examination	4.1	4.2
A need for special assistance for Maori and other Polynesian school students	4.1	1.4
Inclusion of religious education in secondary schools	1.4	1.4
A need for a change in the way subjects are taught	4.1	1.4
A need for new subjects more relevant to the modern world	13.5	15.3

[a] This and subsequent tables have been adapted from those in the 'Interim Report
on Youth Opinion' (Pitt 1970). Numbers are omitted. The sample size was 148,
13 per cent of the total school population.

110 (or nearly 40 per cent) left high school without the minimum qualification of School Certificate. The Youth Opinion Survey suggests that for almost half of those without qualification, they had not fulfilled their own wishes or intentions in this respect.

TABLE 6
POINT OF SCHOOL LEAVING

	%
As soon as I am fifteen	4.0
After three years at school	12.8
After passing School Certificate	33.1
After gaining University Entrance	22.2
After a year in Form 7	18.9
I don't know	8.7

Although the table does not show it, a disproportionate number of those who leave without formal qualifications are Maori and other Polynesian children. Consequently these young people are grossly under-represented in senior forms.

If one considers that School Certificate is becoming increasingly regarded as a prerequisite for entering a skilled trade, then the following table of vocational aspirations also reveals a gap between expectations and fulfilment.

TABLE 7
ACTIVITIES AFTER LEAVING SCHOOL

	%
Look for a job	13.5
Become apprenticed to a trade	18.2
Go on to advanced education	17.5
Seek professional or vocational training (e.g. nursing or teaching, not necessarily at university)	29.7
None of these	10.1

This last table hides a significant difference between the vocational goals of boys and girls. The largest group amongst boys (nearly one third) desired apprenticeship to a trade. The largest group amongst girls (44 per cent) were interested in the professional and semiprofessional vocations.

Given a list of 70 occupations, the high school pupils demonstrated their individuality by not bunching their choices around any single occupation. No occupation scored more than 8 per cent although some cognate occupations together scored relatively well. Of approximately 150 responses, only 8 pupils 'didn't know' what work or career they would like to take up. The favourite occupations were as follows (numbers of responses in brackets): nurse (12) 8 per cent; doctor (10) 6.7 per cent; office worker (9) 6 per cent; primary school teacher (7) 4.7 per cent; mechanic (6) 4 per cent; Army/Armed forces (5) 3.4 per cent.

Airline pilot, commercial traveller, and secretary each drew four responses or 2.7 per cent each. Accountant, carpenter, draughtsman, farmer, fitter and turner, journalist, kindergarten teacher and works manager each drew 3 responses or 2 per cent each. Air hostess, civil engineer, business manager, dental nurse, electrical engineer, forestry worker, hairdresser, high school teacher, laboratory technician, mechanical engineer, merchant navy, navy, physiotherapist, shop assistant, and typist, each drew only 2 responses or 1.3 per cent each.

It is interesting to note that no boy wanted to be a policeman, although 1 girl chose policewoman. More surprising are the single scores for computer-programming and industrial chemist, 2 occupations which are associated with modern expanding industrial enterprise, especially that of the pulp and paper mills. And, only 2 chose 'forestry worker'.

At least one third of the occupations listed would require the person to either be trained or to practice or work in a town or city other than Tokoroa. How do these young people view the prospect of leaving their home town? Nearly one third expected to remain in the town to work. More than half (53 per cent) expected to work or train away from the town. Sixteen per cent did not know (Pitt 1970: 11). For a fairly wide range of skilled trades for boys, and for a wide range of labouring jobs, there is probably sufficient opportunity locally. The trade examination pass list for 1970 included 50 successful local candidates in 14 different trades, from automotive diesel mechanics to timber machining. But only 1 trade that is traditionally a women's one was represented—hair-dressing, with 5 candidates. Work and vocational opportunities for girls leaving school seem to be much more limited. There is some demand for shop and restaurant assistants although girls must compete with married women for these jobs and for the office or clerical jobs around town. In the opinion of the high school principal it is unequal competition, with the majority of those school leavers qualified in commercial practice having to seek work beyond the town (*South Waikato News*, 30 March 1971).

Unfortunate as this situation has been, and still is, it is almost certain that as the town grows in size and in industrial and commercial sophistication, and as the mean age of married couples steadily rises, so the local vocational opportunities for young people will increase. The achievement of city status should give a boost to many forms of enterprise—service, commercial, and industrial.

Meanwhile, young people while still at school play an important part in the economy of the town not only as spenders but as earners. Forty per cent (about 25) of the girls in the youth survey were engaged as part-time shop or restaurant workers at various times throughout the year—after school or during holidays. Boys tended to have a greater spread of occupations such as shop assistant, delivery boy, or lawn mowing. About 40 per cent of all fourth formers were engaged in out-of-school work. By the fifth form this increased to 60 per cent of all students. Boys earned more than girls—nearly one half earned more than $100 per year whereas 60 per cent of the girls earned less than $50 (Pitt 1970: 15–16). As consumers, these young people chose to spend one third of their income on clothes, one fifth on savings, less than one tenth on pop records, the same on sports and sports gear, and only small amounts on food, cinema, books, and transport. Apparently none of them used their money to help out with the family budget. Money represents a measure of independence from the adult world. Income, and the independence it brings, increases markedly over the last few years of schooling.

Meanwhile too, the teenage young are engaged in much of the club or association life of the community. Approximately 70 per cent of the school sample belonged to some kind of club or association—a figure which compares fairly favourably with the ratio of adult joining (see Table 2 page 67). The pattern of preference runs as follows:

TABLE 8
CLUB AFFILIATION

Type	%
Church Youth Club and Bible Class	6.0
Outdoor activities and outdoor sports clubs (e.g. skiing, sailing)	40.5
Indoor games and recreation (e.g. chess, boxing)	9.4
Musical and Drama Clubs	2.7
Youth and Leadership Associations (e.g. Scouts, YMCA)	6.7
Cultural Clubs (e.g. Maori, Polynesian Clubs)	0.6
Community Service Associations (e.g. St Johns, Red Cross)	4.0
Not applicable/don't know	0.6

Boys are generally more avid joiners and their choice of outdoor clubs is more marked than for girls. Incidence of joining also seems to increase with age – even though there are clubs which cater for children of primary school age, notably, Cubs and Brownies, Scouts and Guides, Junior Red Cross, the junior section of St Johns Ambulance, Girls and Boys Life Brigades, junior sections of the Y.M.C.A. and of sports associations – rugby, League and Association (soccer) football, midget and junior Marching Girls, junior tennis, and softball.

The informal social life of the older (high school age) young people points up a first preference for dances, discotheque, and movies – but only for 25 per cent of the sample. There appears no other single activity or group of activities of the informal kind which draws the attention of any more than a small proportion of these young people. The following vignettes, taken from the 'Teen Scene' column in the local newspaper, give some idea of the variety of group life (mostly informal) pursued by the young people. It gives no indication, of course, of those kinds and shades of activity which the adult section of society frowns upon.

A night out on Monday for a group of sixteen Tokoroa teen-agers, who travelled to Tauranga to see a New Zealand indoor basketball team play the visiting American team. Among the group were several high school pupils and ardent basketball fans and players.

Over eighty people gathered on Saturday night to celebrate the
engagement of Christine Smith of Cobham Drive to Karl
Miller, also of Tokoroa. Christine, 17, works in one of the
town's dairies and Karl is employed by N.Z. Forest Products
Limited at Kinleith. The party was held at the home of a family
friend in Arthur Street.

Six Tokoroa High School musicians with plenty of talent have
grouped themselves together to form a band. [They] made their
public debut on Thursday night when they performed at the
Miss Tokoroa High School 1971 Show after only a fortnight
together as a group.

'Doing their thing' next Saturday night will be members of the
Tokoroa Methodist/Presbyterian Bible Class. They've organised
a dance and have invited Bible Classes from Matamata, Te
Aroha, Thames, Hamilton, Melville, Putaruru, and other areas
to come and join in. The evening has no organised programme
and will be a chance for the young folk to 'do their thing'
in their own way.

With Saturday night coming around again soon the newly
formed Tokoroa teen dance committee is in the throes of preparing for another dance, which as usual will be held in the
town's Old Memorial Hall. This will be the third dance they've
organised since they formed the committee.

Playing in a curtain-raiser indoor basketball match at Church
College, Hamilton, last night were members of the Tokoroa
High School Boys A indoor team. Supported by a group of
followers from Tokoroa, they played the first match before a
New Zealand indoor team played against the visiting Americans.

A chilly trip is in store for a group of seventh formers at the
high school next Monday, when they leave for the Chateau at
5 a.m. Organised by Megan Foster and Graham Coleman, the
trip is an annual event, and on the way home the same night,
they plan to stop at De Brett's pools in Taupo for a swim.

The above selection represents teenage life in its more exciting or

stimulating aspects, which include frequent participation in a wide
range of indoor and outdoor sports. Yet, 68 per cent of the pupils
in the 'Youth Opinion Survey' declared that 'provision for youth
interests was not adequate'. More boys (77 per cent) than girls (58
per cent) voiced their dissatisfaction. It is interesting to note here
that *all* the 'lower' fourth formers were dissatisfied. Of the remainder, 24 per cent were satisfied and 7 per cent had no opinion. The
remedies suggested included more evening and social activities
(particularly dances, discotheques, and night clubs), more 'get to-
gethers' and social clubs. (Pitt: 1970: 14).

In pursuing their social life in and beyond the town many young
people use motor vehicles – their parents' cars, chiefly, but many
own motor cycles, motor scooters, or old cars. Predictably, young
people – with a penchant for taking risks and speeding – feature
prominently in the town's accident and death roll. One district
coroner's report declared that 12 out of his 14 inquests, for one
period, were traffic deaths – the average age of the victims being
only 18 years. The worst traffic accident in the town's history
emphasised the mobility and vulnerability of Tokoroa's youth.

The lives of four Tokoroa High School fifth form students were
claimed yesterday in one of the worst motor accidents in the
town's history... All seven occupants of the car had been
playing badminton at the Tokoroa Y.M.C.A. shortly before the
accident. Police believed that the group may have travelled to
Campbell Road... to look at the circuit of last Sunday's teenage
driving contest.

South Waikato News, 1 June 1971

Two sets of responses from the high school pupils reveal something more of the problems which young people face as they
approach adulthood in this town. For the first set, below, pupils
were asked, first, which problem they regarded as the major one
and second, which ones they still regarded as problems but as not
quite so important. Only 14 (9.4 per cent) of the 148 felt there were
no problems.

If the large proportion (40 per cent) of these young people,
chose 'lack of interesting activities' as the 'major problem' and if
theirs is even a roughly accurate appraisal, then the fairly high

rate of choices for 'under age drinking', 'violence', and 'sexual behaviour' as 'major problems' would seem to be all the more credible, although not necessarily as serious as the limited code wording might suggest.

If we now look at the second set of responses, on the question of adult understanding of youth, some sort of youthful 'rebellion' against the authority and standards of adult society would seem inevitable.

TABLE 9
YOUTH OPINIONS ON YOUTH PROBLEMS

Problem	Major Problem %	Secondary Problems	
Sexual behaviour of young people	8.1	20.9	2.7
Theft by young people	5.4	8.1	6.0
Under-age drinking	16.8	19.5	9.4
Young people taking drugs	1.3	4.7	4.7
Violence by young people	13.5	12.1	16.8
Trouble between people of different races	5.4	1.3	4.0
Vandalism by young people	4.0	10.1	11.4
A lack of anything interesting to do for young people	39.8	6.0	12.1

TABLE 10
OPINIONS ON ADULT UNDERSTANDING

Opinion	%
Most adults understand the problems of young people fairly well	13.5
Most adults are out of touch with the problems of young people	25.6
Most adults are unsympathetic to young people	2.7
Most adults have made a mess of the world which the young people will have to clear up	2.7
Most adults would like to help but aren't sure how to go about it	47.9
I don't know anything about this	3.3
None of these statements apply	3.3

Of the many and various forms which youthful 'rebellion' takes in Tokoroa as elsewhere in our society, only the more spectacular, the more serious, or more reprehensible are brought to public attention. The local newspaper, conscientious in most forms of reporting on the town scene, is diligent also in its coverage of local court cases.[5] The following is a fairly representative list of offenses from the court reporting of the South Waikato News, almost any issue of which provides several harrowing, sordid, or sometimes amusing examples:

A 9 year old boy planned a raid on two Tokoroa homes where a total of $146 in goods was stolen, the Tokoroa Children's Court was told on Thursday ... Appearing before the court was a slightly older girl charged with burgling the houses. She said the boy planned the raid.

Two 12 year old Tokoroa boys who entered the Intermediate School and wrote obscenities on the blackboard appeared in the Tokoroa Children's Court on Friday ... The youths could give no particular reason for their actions.

After arriving back in Tokoroa from a football trip a 15 year old boy ransacked the office and seven rooms at the Redwood Park Motel, upturning television sets and furniture before being apprehended when trying to illegally enter a car.

A 15 year old ... pleaded guilty before Mr W.R. Birkes S.M. in the Tokoroa Children's Court on Thursday to having unlawful sexual intercourse with a 14 year old school friend ... The girl's father was charged with having a delinquent child in his care ... The girl was found at a house in Tokoroa in the company of several other girls and youths.

Two fifteen year old members of the Tokoroa 'Dogs' gang were convicted on charges of disorderly behaviour when they appeared before Mr W.R. Birkes S.M. in the Tokoroa Children's Court on Thursday.

A 16 year old Tokoroa youth was fined a total of $25 on two charges of being a minor on licensed premises and $25 for supplying false information to police when he appeared in the Tokoroa Children's Court on Thursday.

A youth who threw a stone at the base of the Rosebery Mall fountain was fined $60 in the Tokoroa Magistrate's Court on Friday.

A 17 year old Tokoroa tree planter was remanded to appear in the Tokoroa Magistrate's Court today for sentence on two charges of theft and one of car conversion.

A youth who urinated against the wheel of a Tokoroa police constable's car at 10.10 p.m. on December 16 was fined $200 when he appeared in the Tokoroa Magistrate's Court on Thursday.

A 17 year old youth who swore at a theatre attendant when she refused to allow his young girl friend admission to see a certificated R18 movie, appeared in the Tokoroa Magistrate's Court last week.

A youth who shouted as a police van passed him in Leith Place was fined $15 when he appeared in the Tokoroa Magistrate's Court yesterday.

A 17 year old Tokoroa youth who pleaded guilty to charges of stealing and using the narcotic Pethedine was granted interim suppression of name in the Tokoroa Magistrate's Court on Thursday.

A youth who threw a pumpkin at a jewellery shop window, and stole a watch and a ring, was placed on probation for 12 months.

The Tokoroa Magistrate's Court was told on Tuesday of how an 18 year old girl smashed a fire detector in the cells of the Tokoroa police station after being found drunk outside the Tokoroa Hotel.

Three Tokoroa youths appeared in the Tokoroa Magistrate's Court yesterday charged with entering Tokoroa Menswear Ltd in Rosebery Street. The shop was entered on the weekend and clothing to the value of $600 was believed to have been stolen.

Young Maori people—boys and young men mainly, but not infrequently girls and young women—feature prominently in these 'offenses' and 'felonies'. Approximately three-quarters of the district probation officer's case load is with young Maori 'offenders'. For reasons already discussed in Chapter 3 this is not surprising. In many ways they are the most alienated members of any urban society in New Zealand. Their youth, their physical Maori identity, their lower educational attainment, their lack of familiarity with European social skills, the often less effective controls from their immediate families—all these work inexorably against many Maori youths. The high rate of 'offensive' behaviour could be regarded as their (unconscious) protest against the dice which are loaded against them, a fundamental fact which magistrates seldom seem to acknowledge.

Yet, Tokoroa cannot be said to be prone to crime and violence— not even at the height of adverse publicity in 1969 and 1970 when gangs of youths gave periodic trouble and when 2 separate murders, beyond the town, were traced to men living in Tokoroa, The local head of police about this time referred to 'a minority element in the town which occasionally gives trouble but this is more in the sphere of disorder and violence rather than actual crime'. And in 1971 the Minister of Justice, while visiting the town, declared publicly that Tokoroa's crime rate was 'nothing out of the ordinary'. If this was and is the case, then it would seem that anxiety for the local social order, and for the town's image, could well be displaced by more active concern for the total needs of youth, and especially Maori youth, in the town.

Finally, in this sketch of young people in Tokoroa, there is evidence of their concern for social problems in and beyond the town and their willingness to speak out and to act on their own behalf. A numerical minority perhaps, but their significance would seem undiminished. When asked whether they themselves or some (named) category of persons or institutions should organize youth activities, nearly a third chose 'young people themselves', nearly a quarter chose 'the Church', 11 per cent chose 'interested adults' and 9 per cent chose service organizations (e.g.

Jaycees). No one thought school teachers should run organizations for youth! (Pitt 1970: 13). And among the encouraging signs of debate and active concern are the following, gleaned from local newspaper items (1971). Not all are quoted verbatim.

'Teenagers to Discuss Problems'—of lack of entertainment facilities etc. in the town—in the Methodist Church Hall on Sunday. All are welcome to this meeting, convened by the Methodist Church Bible Class and Catholic Youth Group. The Y-teens and Rotoract are specifically invited.

The High School student council work project is in full swing this week. It is aiming to collect $2000 for the building of a school swimming pool to be ready for the 1972–73 season. All types of jobs will be carried out by the students. (By Thursday of that week $1500 had been gained.)

Seventh Formers at the High School organise the school's annual swimming sports for the third year in succession, and, this year for the first time the 'Miss Tokoroa High School' contest will be organised by a committee of 12 fifth formers, who are conducting the contest as a class project to raise $100 for the school's swimming pool fund.

The inaugural meeting has been held for a new young peoples club—The Timberland Teens' comprised of members of the Y.M.C.A. or sons and daughters of Y's men. The first chairman is a 17 year old. 'I'm sure that every body wants to belong to something,' he said 'and we could have the beginnings of a great club here.' The idea grew out of a Y.M.C.A. family camp at Wanganui where the young people undertook to organise entertainment for younger children.

Students of the Tokoroa High School now have the chance to publicly express their opinions at regular intervals. A Speaker's stand has been erected outside the college hall and each Friday anyone who is a little 'hot under the collar' about an issue of any description can stand up and 'let off steam' to the audience. The public discussions have so far proved very successful ...
'Originators [were] a sixth form class who put the suggestion to the student council.'

The Tokoroa County Borough Committee has issued a permit
to a group of Tokoroa High School pupils to stage a mobilisation
march protesting against the Viet Nam war in the town
tomorrow night ... despite strong opposition from parents.

A 'Happening' in the town? Councillor Foote says he supports
the idea. At other Happenings he saw only lots of young people
enjoying themselves. Council debates and approves, on condition that the Parks and Reserves Committee, and the police,
'give their sanction'. (They did, and the first Happening drew
three to four hundred young people. The last, before winter,
drew 600).

The last three items would seem especially significant. They
are signs that Tokoroa is 'growing up', mellowing, becoming more
sensitive, more 'tuned in' to the wider world and that some at
least of the town's youth are promoting and advancing this process.
At the same time they are expressing their right to be heard, and
the right to 'do their own thing'. It is unfortunate perhaps that
the most concerned and active of these young people will leave the
town to pursue careers and to live permanently in other places.

NOTES

1 From an interview in the N.Z. *Listener*, 20 January 1967.
2 This was in 1971. It was estimated that the figure would climb to 670 births per
   year by mid-1974, thus maintaining a rate of increase by local births of rather
   more than $3\frac{1}{2}$ per cent—a figure which would be matched, or exceeded, by the
   immigration of people of all ages—including children.
3 See Forster and Ramsay (1969) for a full discussion of this 'cycle' as it affects
   Maori people. Also John E. Watson's perceptive study, *Horizons of Unknown
   Power* (1967).
4 Derogatory opinion on the quality of teaching and academic standards, made or
   suggested by anxious or snobbish parents who send (or might wish to send) their
   children 'out' to school, appears to have little foundation in fact. The pass rates in
   public examinations—for School Certificate, University Entrance, Bursary, and
   Scholarship—all seem satisfactory by national standards.
5 This newspaper, otherwise excellent, follows the widespread fashion and function
   of being an instrument of shame, and thereby of injustice, to persons charged
   and convicted of almost any offense. The names of offenders (unless they are
   children) are almost invariably published—along with any 'newsworthy' feature
   of their offense.

Houses, Streets, and   6
Neighbours

I'm not sure if this particular street is unique but the amount of interaction is negligible ... The extent appears to be only 'cross-fence', ... all residents appear to be able to say 'hello' to their neighbour but this seems to be the extent of the exchange for many.

excerpt from a neighbourhood study

... maybe I am terribly lucky in having such marvellous neighbours, ready to help out with concreting paths, putting up the fences etc. The area is rich in friendship as well as a mixture of nationalities. Everyone appears to get on extremely well one with the other.

excerpt from a neighbourhood study

This chapter has been written, for the most part, by residents themselves as it consists mainly of neighbourhood studies presented by people who took part in the 1970 Community Study Workshop in Tokoroa (see Chapter 8). Space permits the inclusion of only 6 of these, and then only excerpts, chosen to depict various kinds of neighbourhoods and various attitudes to life in these neighbourhoods.[1] There are no studies of neighbourhoods composed of 'privately' built homes, either in the older section of the town on rising ground to the west of the business centre, or in newer 'higher class' areas such as that on the north-west margin of the town. However, company-built housing is still the majority type in Tokoroa.

'Neighbourhood', for the purpose of these studies, is only very loosely defined, and may or may not be a fairly discrete or bounded group of households. If the resident lives in a cul-de-sac (and there are many in Tokoroa) the neighbourhood will be relatively well defined spatially. But if on a continuous street, the person will define neighbourhood more in terms of a pattern of social interaction (no matter how superficial) based upon his or her own awareness and knowledge of other householders in the vicinity. The definition of neighbourhood then becomes quite relative; it depends upon the position of the observer.

There is no description of the writer of the first study. The second author is male and European; the third a Pakeha woman; the fourth a Maori woman; the fifth a young wife of English birth, and the sixth a young Pakeha woman. All except the last were married and resident in Tokoroa at the time of writing. All used a guidesheet or framework to assist them with their descriptions but were invited to treat their subject freely (and some did). They were asked not to seek new information from neighbours but to use the knowledge and insights already gained from living in their neighbourhood. (The author of the sixth study used her parents to augment her own knowledge.) Except that they have been cut, the texts are as they were written by the residents.

CASE STUDY 1

Ours is a street for through traffic but not heavy traffic. It is a N.Z. Forest Products housing area. There is no playing space for children in the immediate area but a semi-developed area 500 metres away. The school is 800 metres, kindergarten just over 1 kilometre, the town (shopping centre) 1.5 kilometres away.

The street is 17 years old. There has been a considerable turnover of residents. All the husbands work at N.Z. Forest Products, half being shift workers. Half the people are New Zealanders, the rest are Dutch, British, and Samoan. All are in the 25 to 45 year age group except one older household. Occupancy in the neighbourhood ranges from 16 years to 2 years, with an average of 7 years. Children range from 6 months to 16 years with an average age of 8 years.

There is very little mixing in the neighbourhood. We have very little contact; a neighbour on one side collects mail when we are away and occasionally borrows something. (The borrowing is occasional because he is well set up). The neighbourhood is quiet and we like it that way. Our social contacts are now all outside the neighbourhood. Previously we have been very friendly with neighbours but these people have left . . . but we still maintain contact.

We have teenage children and now take less interest in children's activities which, in the past were a source of contact. My interests outside the neighbourhood bring us our social contacts e.g. clubs and cultural groups ... Earlier contact between people in the neighbourhood could take place at P.T.A. (Parent Teacher Association) type meetings, but these were obligation meetings rather than interest meetings. With older children our meetings are more of the type of things we wish to attend. We, both husband and wife, are working.

CASE STUDY 2

I live in a small 'place' [a cul-de-sac, banjo-shaped in this case] consisting of 18 company-owned houses, all of which are 5 years old ... senior staff houses interspersed with standard type houses. The street has been designed on the 'open-range' principle with dividing fences around the back half only, with no dividing lines at all in the front, creating a park-like effect. I think this gives a very pleasant appearance to the street as well as creating a good playing area for children. Very few residents object to other's children playing on or crossing their front lawns. The actual road itself is quite safe for small children ...

Being the longest resident in the street I have seen many houses occupied and re-occupied. Most of the residents that have left have done so to better themselves at their occupation. Two families have left to return to their countries of origin (Scotland and Australia). Only 1 family to my knowledge has left because they did not like Tokoroa, after 2 years residence ...

When we moved in there was only 1 house already occupied and it took some 2 months for the whole street to be filled.

We very soon got to know the first people in the street and found we had very much in common ... As they lived 3 doors away we met, through them, their new neighbours and they ours and so on ... We met a number of new arrivals through having to help extricate cars, moving vans and trailers that had got bogged.

As time progressed the menfolk especially got to know each other during the course of laying lawns and setting up gardens, etc. This, I think, was a very good thing as since then people have moved into houses that have grounds already established and started living their own lives without any necessary recourse to neighbours. Of the 18 houses in the street, there are only 5 of the original residents left; these 5 are still very good friends and neighbours, although nowadays there is very little house visiting done.

For the first 18 months the wives especially were gathering together for coffee or evenings quite a lot. Most of them had come here from other places and other countries and were possibly homesick and hungry for companionship. As a result of this visiting some petty squabbles broke out. A might have offended B and wasn't talking or some such thing. B and C may not be on talking terms with E which made it awkward if you happened to be D and friendly with A,B,C, and E. As time passed by, people moved away and new people came in. As each successive family arrived we discovered we did not even know the people who had left let alone the new arrivals.

Friendships started to spread out further afield. We met people through different organizations and found we did not need contact with the people in our street and as this happened with all the families, petty squabbles and such stopped completely and now a very good, harmonious existence has come about.

Of the 5 families that have remained here for 5 years, 3 are senior staff and 2 are tradesmen . . . I think that the mixing up of senior staff personnel with other workers has a very good effect on the community as a whole. It tends to break down the class distinction that could arise, and makes for a better understanding of each other's work problems. I find that being a shift worker amongst a small community of non-shift workers presents no problems at all. Most near neighbours are aware of my sleeping times and go out of their way to avoid waking me.

In this street we have 5 different designs of houses—3 senior staff types and 2 for other workers. Senior staff houses are all three-bedroomed and of a reasonable size, although the bedrooms are slightly too small. Construction is of a type totally unsuited for our climate and are of a generally unimaginative shape. The siting of the houses is extremely poor and little attempt has been made to build or place a house to catch the sun.

Ordinary type houses although smaller than staff houses are no more cosy or comfortable . . . the construction is unsuited for this climate and because of poor choice of material and poor workmanship they are nothing more than ice-boxes in winter. Most of them are situated in such a manner that bedrooms get no sun at all in winter. The general appearance of these houses is dreadful and is very similar to State Housing schemes. . . twenty years ago.

CASE STUDY 3

Our neighbourhood is a fairly new area—5 years old—all company houses, some small, some larger. Our house is on a corner section and the street is a no-exit 'place'. The house is of a larger style but not well placed for sun, and bathroom and toilets face the main road . . . Otherwise it suits us fine as it has a good sized living area. Some houses are owned by the families and these all have lovely gardens; ours and others about tend to be rather barren. . . There is no through traffic, so it's reasonably safe for children to wander about and they mix freely. The only house I have 'over the fence' access to is next door and inhabited by Islanders who seem to speak little English. There are 3 children. The woman will smile and say 'hello'; the men look the other way. . .

[Our] arrival here was not exactly tinged with pleasure. Tokoroa was the only place with a suitable job available at the time. We were prepared to stay a few years while the children got through the baby stages.

Nobody approached the house the first few days. I unpacked on my own as [my husband] was working straight away. Our son went straight over the road to Mrs F (for friend) where there was a boy the same age, a younger girl, and a baby boy. He also met the other children from round about. He is a gregarious child. . . He 'lived' across the road and on the third day I went across to apologise to Mrs F for his intrusion and was greeted pleasantly and we have been good friends ever since, able to call on each to mind kids, etc. Her husband is a shift worker so has lots of day hours at home.

Two weeks later Mrs F introduced me to Mrs E (for English) by arranging for us to go there for morning tea. We went, children and all, and it was harrowing – a very 'precise' house, nice things everywhere and both Mrs F and myself trying to control children and not able to enjoy conversation. . . I asked her back here for morning tea a week after the first visit. . . Later, when my baby was born she visited me in the annexe. . .

Gradually over the past 12 months I have gotten to know the faces of other immediate neighbours but there has been *no* contact! . . . A couple of months ago a Dutch girl moved [into the neighbourhood], obviously from some other part of Tokoroa as they took weeks to shift everything. When I realised they were living there I went across, said 'hello', introduced myself etc., made a date for a 'cuppa' and now she will pop in occasionally and may be termed an acquaintance.

Another couple moved in behind us 2 weeks ago. I saw her in the garden and made an approach. She comes in to use the phone, says 'hello' etc., but no further contact yet.

Now that my second boy is 8 months old I am starting to get away from my immediate environment. I don't find it easy because of household pressure, but feel the need for personal contact outside my family very greatly ... There seems to be plenty of scope in the town but when time is precious I want to do something worthwhile. I tried evening pottery classes for a while earlier on but was too tired to concentrate at night. I found the women there very friendly, so may return in the near future. When my first boy starts school I want to help with P.T.A. and possibly even school committee. Plunket and kindergarten organisations leave me cold! Also League of Mothers or Jaycettes. Later I would like to rejoin the Guiding movement, but this is all in the future. At present I get pleasure from work friends my husband brings home, visiting friends and relations from other towns, and weekend day trips in surrounding countryside and the occasional week or so back home in Wellington.

Interaction between families round about seems to be limited to the children – although some women appear to talk over the fence and some men chat on the sidewalk on their way home from work. All the families except for 2 'new settlers' have been here 2 years or more. Most seem to exist as families. One is visited by other family members a lot. The rest, I don't know how they are placed for friends; they must have them. The Islanders next door have weekend visitors who appear to be single men; they drink a lot at these times.

I would like to know the people about me better, but I can see this is going to take a long time. I feel the best way to get to know people here in Tokoroa is to join an organisation and make the effort oneself.

CASE STUDY 4

This study is of an older established area. It is not a cul-de-sac. The houses line a 'through' street near the point of intersection with a fairly busy traffic route. All the houses on the street are Forest Products owned. Two (of the dozen or so) have been bought by people occupying them. On one side we have an old couple who have been here for about 14 years. Across the road is another old couple who have been here for just over 14 years. Others along the street have been here for from 3 months to about 10 years.

There is a playing area behind the kindergarten [nearby] but it is rarely used by children in the neighbourhood. People use it for walking dogs; there is no play equipment. Cars drive down the alleyway (off this street). Both sides of the alleyway are fenced and if children should be caught there by a car they would have no place to go to get out of the way... Children have to play in their own back yards.

Mr and Mrs A: Elderly couple on their own, family grown up with children of their own. The husband works at Kinleith and is a shift worker... They live away a lot; have a bach at the beach. They are on speaking terms with us. Both pakeha.

Mr and Mrs B: Husband on day shift ... a Kiwi[2], with a Maori wife [the author of the study] and 6 children ... Have lived here for 4 years. Try to get out and mix with others. Eldest daughter—8 years—goes to Y.M.C.A. and Brownies ... They all go away to play at other homes if I know where they are going ...

Mr and Mrs C: Husband works with my husband ... he is in his mid-40s and is a Kiwi. His wife, mid-30s, is a Maori. They have been here about 4½ years and are buying the house they are in from NZ Forest Products. They have 3 daughters ... This family is a bit reserved but mix quite well with others in the street now. They go away for most holidays or long weekends.

Mr and Mrs? [name not known to author] have rented the house from owners ... Own a business in town. Don't mix well with neighbours.

Mr and Mrs D: Husband on shift work; a Samoan. Wife a pakeha. Have a year old baby. Husband's aunt and cousin live with them. Aunt looks after the baby when Mrs D is teaching and aunt works part-time at Kinleith (in the evenings). Cousin works at the post office in town. All get on quite well with neighbours; say hello and usually have a friendly chat.

Mr and Mrs E: Husband a shift worker; an Australian. Wife a Maori. Both in 30s. No children. Have been here about 3½ years. Mrs E works as a nurse in Tokoroa Hospital. Very nice, friendly couple. Always say hello or if children and I are down town they bring us home.

Mr and Mrs F: Husband a shift worker, both Samoans. Have 3 boys . . . Have been here over 4 years. Always say hello when I meet them.

Mr and Mrs G: Husband a shift worker. Both pakeha. Lived here about 14 years. In early 50s. Grown up children with families of their own. They mix quite well with others in the street. They get away quite a lot (have a bach at the beach).

Mr and Mrs H: Husband works from 7 a.m. to 4.30 p.m. Both are Maori, in their 30s. Wife works as a nurse in the hospital. They have 2 daughters . . . Have lived here for 3 years. They mix well with others in the neighbourhood.

Mr and Mrs I: Husband a shift worker. Both Maori. Have 5 children. Husband in his 30s; wife mid-20s. Have been here about 3 years. They stick more to their own family, but also very friendly with neighbours. Tend to be on the borrowing side . . .

Mr and Mrs J: Husband a shift worker, a Kiwi. Wife an Australian. Have 2 small sons . . . Have been here 5 or 6 years. They lead a sporting life e.g. badminton, keep-fit classes. Social life is Workingman's Club.

Mr and Mrs K: Husband a shift worker. Both Kiwis. Have a 16 year old daughter working in a shop in town. Wife works part-time at Kinleith. . . Both in early 40s. Away a lot but friendly with neighbours.

Mr and Mrs L: Husband a shift worker. I think they are both Kiwis. A young couple in early 20s. Have a 6 month old son. Fairly new arrivals—have been here about a year. A friendly couple who get on with neighbours.

Mr and Mrs M: Husband a shift worker. Both Maori in late 30s, early 40s. Have a 17 years old daughter (away, training to be a nurse) and 2 younger sons. At the moment they have Mrs M's mother staying with them. An easy couple to get on with. Have been here about a year.

The age groups tend to stick together though they have quite a lot to do with others on the street. The older ones with grown up families and grandchildren sort of keep together. The others with children more or less of the same age groups tend to spend more time together.

I baby sit for most mothers on the street at one time or other. I baby sit for the woman next door, and next term I shall be looking after Mrs H's 2 children from across the road. Last

Christmas I had Mrs I's 3 children. Mrs H has looked after my children a couple of times. Mrs M has looked after my children. I've minded Mrs J's 2 boys. Mrs I borrows from me and also from Mrs H.

A recent bereavement on the street had some of the neighbours, who don't normally speak together, help one another in that a few ladies did some baking for the widow of the deceased. And a christening at our place had the neighbours next door meeting a lot of the others on the street.

Our neighbourhood isn't really too bad to live in—only there doesn't seem to be any place for the children to play together, unless they play in someone's back yard... There are no other opportunities for people to get to know each other better unless they are prepared to join a sports group or to enrol children in kindergarten or playcentre.

CASE STUDY 5

This is by a young English born wife of a professional employee of N.Z. Forest Products. She had not been married long and was relatively new to Tokoroa. We live in a housing area erected by N.Z. Forest Products for its employees. As group housing areas go this is a good one. The houses are spacious (3 bedrooms), and light. They are built on small sections and they all have a back section behind the houses. Because of the smallness of the sections the closeness to other neighbours can sometimes be disconcerting to me as I like, and have previously had, relative seclusion. The area where we live is new, very new,—only a few houses away the workmen are putting the finishing touches to other houses and at the end of our street there is a whole batch of houses in the early stages of construction. Because of the newness of the area we are still luckily surrounded by paddocks but judging by recent bulldozing and tree felling this will not be for long. As Kinleith is expanding Tokoroa expands and this sort of thing is inevitable.

Gardens vary greatly in this area. The people at the far end of the street who have been here the longest have lawns and the odd shrub. The newer people have lawns rolled, planted, and are now waiting for results, and the remainder, whether they be long-time occupants or newly arrived ones, have erected a mental block between them and their barren patches of lawn (weeds) that surround them and show no inclination to break down the barrier. We fall into this last category.

Playgrounds of the municipal sort are non-existent in this area and are very scarce in Tokoroa. The nearest 'park' that I can think of is at the other end of Balmoral Drive, about 3 kilometres away and this is a grassy area about the size of 2 football fields. We are surrounded by paddocks, as I said, but the children don't really seem to play on them at all. In fact the only area where I've seen children playing is around the bulldozed areas, sliding down the large piles of earth left when the top soil is removed from the new sections [a common practice]. The road is of no special importance. It is not a main one so there is not a real problem. Most of the traffic occurs at the weekends when couples drive around to look at the new houses. There are always buses on the road but these are N.Z. Forest Products buses taking employees to Kinleith. They start at about 6 a.m. and continue to about 12 p.m. Because of the shift work they are both fetching and carrying at odd hours throughout the day and night. There is a town bus run but it doesn't pass this way . . .

As far as I can observe, interaction in my neighbourhood in Tokoroa is rare. Family units stick pretty much to themselves after having felt obliged to make themselves known to their neighbours. Borrowing the legendary 'cup of sugar' seems non-existent. Children do play together but in my opinion it is the school that brings them together rather than the neighbourhood. Why is this so? I will have to speak wholly for myself—why I have not tried to get to know my neighbours. Shyness has a little to do with it perhaps, but it is by no means the main reason. Laziness and inertia would have more to do with it I think. Being newly married I am still enjoying living just with my husband—getting to know him and becoming adjusted to him. We have enough friends, mainly those my husband made before we were married, to keep us occupied and happy. I don't feel like exerting myself to make friends. As far as I'm concerned it takes a fair amount of effort to get to know a complete stranger. You never really get to know their interests: and why because they live next door does this necessarily mean they share your interests? Speaking wholly for myself, I would rather retain my privacy than have to spend my time being polite to people.

So far no occasions have brought the neighbourhood together or blown it apart. The only snags and worries about living in this neighbourhood exist in my own mind. Lack of female companionship worries me sometimes but not enough to make me seek out my neighbours. I have the companionship of my husband and our friends and during the day I enjoy being by myself—having time to read what I like, to do what I like. Also, I regard the situation I am in a temporary one both in the fact that soon I will have my baby to occupy me and that in about 2 years or less we will be going to England.

How much do I depend on social contacts outside my neighbourhood? Only a small amount. This is not surprising because as I am new to Tokoroa I have very few social contacts. I enjoy seeing the people that I know but I wouldn't say that I actually depended on them to a great extent. The only people that I really depend on are my immediate family, my husband, my parents in Hamilton. I have not made friends in Tokoroa that are close enough for me to depend on them.

I think that there would be greater opportunities to meet people through children. Places that children attend with their parents—for instance, play centres and school events, would make for closer communication between parents and, in some cases, neighbours. In a few weeks time I am starting at the ante-natal clinic at the local hospital and I will look with interest to see if this makes any changes to my life as it is at the moment. Also I think that husbands bring families together because of working ties. This is because most people work for the same employer [N.Z. Forest Products] but this tends to favour prejudices through jobs e.g. a bush worker would not get to know an office worker because of his job and vice versa. This would tend to lead to social stratification.

A conclusion is a hard thing to draw on the quality of one's life and of the lives of those around you. When 'quality of life' is mentioned I think immediately of cultural things, art galleries, music, etc. and Tokoroa rates well down in these aspects. Aside from this I would say that most people around Tokoroa could benefit from a rise in the quality of life, not only in the cultural aspect because that is not everybody's cup of tea, and I should think that in Tokoroa the people who feel the need for that sort of thing would be in the minority. No, I mean that a few more parks, a few more trees, a bit more town planning would benefit the town and its inhabitants a great deal. The one over-riding thought that I have when I think of Tokoroa is what a really ugly town it is. Because of this I think people tend to shut themselves up in their houses and make them beautiful and in this way forget about the ugliness outside. Tokoroa is a town without a character as yet. Her population is transient and therefore it is hard for her to make a character that will last. The feeling that I get about Tokoroa is that it is just one big ugly hostel. Housing people because they are at that time working for N.Z. Forest Products and tomorrow or the next day they will be gone and who cares. The idea that anybody would want to live in Tokoroa for a long time, to raise a family here and retire here to me seems incredible. To me and my husband, as to many other people who live here, Tokoroa is just a stepping stone, a gateway to better things where you can come and work for a couple of years, get good money, and then leave it again. Take what you want and go and don't bother about putting back anything worthwhile. This is the attitude of the main percentage of the population and this to my mind is why Tokoroa will never be anything more than a N.Z. Forest Product's 'hostel'.

CASE STUDY 6

This excerpt, too, is from a study by a young woman, but one who spent her teen years in Tokoroa, living with her family in this neighbourhood. A certain unformity characterizes the neighbourhood. Three-bedroom wooden houses built by N.Z. Forest Products are set facing towards the road in one-fifth acre [.08 hectare] sections. Fences of wire-netting strung across wooden posts mark off the side and back boundaries of the sections. Concrete drives lead up to pairs of adjoining garages at the back of each section. This is a factor influencing the amount of interaction between neighbours for they are bound to see each other during their arrivals and departures from the home and when collecting the mail from the letterbox. The street is a dead-end one with a traffic roundabout at the end. Grass and a small tree are planted on it (by N.Z. Forest Products). This area is too small to be used by children for playing on. The footpath is concrete with a grass verge on either side. Each household has taken responsibility for mowing the grass in front of its section, and those at the end of the street take turns mowing the roundabout. This is an unspoken agreement. If a man is mowing his own lawn and sees that the round about needs doing, he does it. The neighbours notice that this is done and feel responsible for sharing in this work. The street is a fairly quiet and safe one, the main traffic being residents and their visitors. Parents do not worry about their children playing close to the road or on the footpath but the younger children are discouraged from actually playing on the road. Occasionally older children may use the road as a tennis court or trolley racing track. Attractive laminated wood lamp-posts are spaced regularly along the street. All electricity and tele-phone wiring is underground. Some residents have devoted considerable time and energy to work on their section in attempts to beautify and to provide themselves with a greater measure of privacy. Their efforts have included landscaping, terracing, put-ting in rock gardens, shrubs, trellises, and sunporches. Pride in the garden appears to be related to the length of residence and whether the house is owned or rented by the family. There are 2 sizes of house and a number of different designs. Initially they were all owned and built by N.Z. Forest Products and they are occupied by their employees who may either rent or buy them.

Mr and Mrs A are New Zealanders (Pakeha) both aged 44 years. They have lived in the neighbourhood for 7 years—since develop-ment and building of the area was first completed. Mr A is a tech-nical manager at N.Z. Forest Products and travels to work by private car. They have 6 children. The eldest—the writer of this report—is a girl aged 19 ... the youngest a boy of 9 ... There is considerably more interaction in the neighbourhood by the children, especially the younger ones playing with neighbouring children, than by Mr and Mrs A whose attitude is that you do not socialize just for the sake of socializing. At home they pursue their interests; gardening, sewing, building a carport and boat. One-day family outings are quite frequent and include visiting the wife's parents, picnics, hot baths [thermal pools] or yachting ... Apart from this the family's main interaction outside the home is through clubs and committees ...

Mr and Mrs B are New Zealanders (Pakeha) aged about 40 years. Mr B is a charge hand at the mill ... Mrs B works at the grocery store [a few blocks away] 3 days each week. They have lived here for 7½ years. Their 2 children both live away from home (1 in Auckland, 1 in Australia) ... Mr and Mrs B spend most of their non-working hours at home ... work in the garden

... joinery and cabinet making ... knitting and sunbathing ...
Mr B occasionally goes to one of the men's clubs for a drink ...
They occasionally visit relatives in Auckland at weekends...

Mr C is Irish, his wife English, and their 3 children were born
in New Zealand. Mr C has a clerical job with N.Z. Forest Products
while Mrs C is part-owner and manager of a ... shop in town.
They are in their early 40s. They have lived in the neighbourhood
only a few months but have lived in Tokoroa for over 10 years ...
Very little is seen of Family C about the neighbourhood... The
family plays an active part in the Operatic Society which involves
them throughout the year.

The D family came to New Zealand from Samoa over 10 years
ago. They were all recently made naturalized New Zealanders.
Mr D's job involves shiftwork at the paper mill. He is about 50
years old ... there are about 8 children, 4 of whom live at home
... the eldest 4 are all married and living in Tokoroa. There is a
lot of visiting and cars coming and going, particularly as all the
boys have cars. Mr A does not remember ever having seen
Mrs D.

The E family: Mr and Mrs A have little knowledge of the E
family. They are probably Maori and the parents are aged 40 to 50
years. They have lived in the neighbourhood for 7 years and have
6 children ... They have a nice garden.

Mr and Mrs F have worked in Australia and are either Australians or New Zealanders. They are aged about 35 years. Mr F is an
... engineer. They have lived in the neighbourhood for 3 years
... the eldest boy is 7... Mr A and Mr F share similar interests
and have a friendly relationship but most of their meetings and
interaction are outside the neighbourhood; for example, Mr A and
Mr F meet while watching their sons play soccer on Saturday
mornings...

Mr and Mrs H are Maoris aged about 40 years. Mr H is a
labourer at the ... mill. They have lived here for $7\frac{1}{2}$ years. In
previous years there have been a number of children here but now
there is only 1 ... he has been in trouble with the police ... Mrs A
discourages her children from playing with him. Mr and Mrs H go
to the pub often. They are not often seen by the A family even
though their place is clearly visible to them. They used to have
noisy parties ... which annoyed the A's and the B's. However,
these ceased with introduction of 10 o'clock hotel closing and may

also have been affected by the opening of a tribal hall in the district.

The I's are New Zealanders (Pakehas) aged 25 to 30 years and have lived in the neighbourhood for 2 years. Mr I is a shiftworker and is probably a tradesman ... there are 4 children ... They have a German Shepherd which ... frightens the neighbouring children if it is annoyed. Mr I's sisters who live in Tokoroa are often there visiting. His hobby is stock cars, both building and driving them. He is often seen working on a car in the driveway or on the road.

Mr and Mrs J are Maoris aged 35 to 40 years. He is from a wealthy farming family and owns land. He is a clerk with N.Z. Forest Products. They have lived in the neighbourhood for less than a year. There are 3 children — 2 of high school age. Mrs A has seen baby clothes on the line and wonders if Mrs J looks after someone else's child, has adopted one, or takes in washing ... Mr J smokes cigars, plays golf a bit, and likes a beer at the men's club. According to Mr A they 'live less like Maoris than other Maoris'.

Family K are New Zealanders (Pakeha) in their early 30s. Mr K is a ... mechanic who works shifts ... They have lived here for 7 years, and have 4 children... The K's don't seem to go out much, possibly to the pub sometimes. Mr K spends his spare time fixing other peoples cars for them or buying and selling cars. He is teaching himself Japanese by records in order to prevent boredom. Mrs K plays badminton and netball. They are building a house at present at the other side of town.

Some appreciation of the quantity and quality of neighbourhood interaction may be gained from my descriptions above. The extent of family A's knowledge of their neighbours is indicated by the differing degrees of fullness of description and is related to the degree of interaction with them. Mr and Mrs A seldom talk to most of their neighbours or even have occasion to say hello to them. There are some whom they have never met or even seen, though the latter is rare. The greatest amount of inter-action is with the 2 families on either side of them—families B and F. These are the only families with whom Mr and Mrs A hold conversations over the fence, or with whom they lend and borrow goods.

The lives of most of the people in the neighbourhood are

centred round their home and family. Neighbourliness and community life are relatively unimportant except in the cases of family H and perhaps C.

When one compares Family A with the 3 families with which it has the most interaction, certain factors emerge as being particularly relevant. Amount of interaction and proximity are correlated in a one to one relationship. Similar social status, as evidenced by occupational status, size of house, and ownership of home appears to be the second major factor. Considered together, these 2 factors appear to account fairly well for the pattern of interaction between family A and its neighbours. Pride in the garden appears to be closely associated to the status variable. It is notable also that most social interaction is with families of the same race, though whether this factor is important or is a matter of chance in this case is difficult to say. It is probably relevant in so far as it affects the social status factor...

Perhaps the earliest spontaneous response of residents to their new environment of the timber town or settlement, is in forms of neighbourhood co-operation. Some Tokoroa residents of long standing testify to a lively spirit of comradeship and mutual aid among neighbours when the town was at an earlier stage of development. It seems that as new residential areas were established it was possible to achieve a similar spirit, at least for a while. One resident describes this for his street or place (Case Study 2). This example is instructive for its suggestion that mutual problems requiring practical and immediate attention may evoke a collective response out of which friendships often develop, and second, for the suggestion that wider (or even extra–) community relationships of friendship and common club membership may gradually displace the more local ones of neighbourhood. (See also Case Study 1, where the facts of neighbours leaving, and of children growing up, are offered as partial explanation for the diminishing contact.) The latter may not always be true for all members of a local neighbourhood, however. Case Study 4 illustrates the closeness and catholicity of social exchange between a woman resident and many of the dozen or so families in her immediate locality. She babysits for other mothers and her home is a focal point for the meeting of children and also of mothers who might not otherwise get to know one another. The woman is thus one of that significant class of neighbourhood 'mediators' who help stimulate mutual knowledge, mutual enjoyment, and also mutual aid amongst residents in times of crisis. Mrs F (for 'Friend') in Study 3 is also a 'mediator' in this sense.

With the scattered and inconclusive evidence on hand it would appear that, with time, neighbourhood localities acquire degrees of impersonality, so that people moving in might find it increasingly difficult to make easy and frequent contact with surrounding residents. The 1969 Survey data (Pitt and Swain 1970: 39–41) tends to support this conclusion. 62 per cent of one sample indicate that they never go visiting locally, although a half may 'drop in occasionally' on neighbours. Only 1 in 10 may 'drop in occasionally' on neighbours in the evening. Less than 1 in 6 do small favours and services for neighbours. One in 7 would take personal troubles to neighbours. This and other evidence suggests that at least a sizeable minority of Tokoroa residents (and possibly a majority) have minimal day to day social contact with their neighbours.

Case studies 3 and 5 portray someting of the 'inner drama' of adjusting oneself to neighbourhood life. They bring out the less obvious dimensions of personality that reach beyond age, social class, and ethnicity and give added meaning to these factors. The last study attempts to explain neighbourhood social exchange (although very modestly) in terms of a combination of factors other than personality. The suggestion that close propinquity plus common occupational status promote, or at least permit, easy social exchange is plausible but not complete; the differences between sociable and not so sociable neighbours and neighbourhoods cannot be contained so neatly (nor would that writer make such a claim). The ethnic factor complicates the picture still further. There seems to be some truth in the suggestion, again put forward by the writer of the last case study, that where race is linked with occupational status it will affect neighbourhood exchange. In the neighbourhood of Study 4, there are as many, if not more, Maori and Pacific Island people than Europeans, and all husbands are of approximately equivalent occupational status. From that writer's description, it would seem that in all ways exchange is more open than in the neighbourhood of Study 6. However the evidence is far too sparse to allow of firm generalisation. Much more data needs to be collected from actual neighbourhoods, and especially from non-European residents. Autobiographical studies are especially valuable because they reveal not only the structural features of personal social network, membership in clubs, etc., but many dynamic cultural facts about the people involved and, perhaps most significant of all, their attitudes, values, hopes, fears, and frustrations. Neighbourhoods might be 'dormitories' for the men, but they are important daily social fields for women and children.

NOTES

1 Several very full and excellent studies made by social science students (ex-Tokoroa residents) have had to be excluded from this selection mainly because of the difficulty in abridging them, but I would like to acknowledge their value for this whole study.

2 Kiwi: a New Zealand-born European, elsewhere referred to in this work as a 'Pakeha'.

3 Charge hand: this position is one step below foreman.

Who's Running this Town? 7

The 'dyarchy' of a County Borough. Political issues, personalities, and political 'apathy'. The 1971 elections.

Local body administration in Tokoroa is concerned with the many practical problems affecting the town, especially the provision of basic services and amenities. But against this scenario of mundane affairs—questions of priorities, and means and costs— there is the drama of local body politics. Central to this drama are complex issues and principles, the clash of personalities, and, to a lesser extent (or less obviously), wider political party influences.

Until 1953 the administration of Tokoroa was the direct responsibility of the Matamata County Council. In that year it became a County Town with a Town Committee. The Committee was constituted partly by popular election of members and partly by nomination of members by the company whose capital was invested so heavily in both industry and town.

In 1966 a special act of parliament, the Tokoroa Empowering Act, created Tokoroa as the first County Borough in New Zealand, with a popularly elected Borough Committee and a Mayor. It appears that this was make-shift legislation—necessary because the older and more cumbersome Counties Act could no longer do justice to Tokoroa's special needs; nor could it be quickly and easily amended to do so. Moreover, it also seems that the special act conferred only limited advantages upon this burgeoning town. County legislation, county administration, and county politics were pervasive (and still are, at the time of writing). For there is not 1 council body responsible for the administration of Tokoroa but 2—the Borough Committee of 10 elected townspeople and the County Council which is responsible for 12 rural ridings of which Tokoroa and its environs is only one.[1] This is the 'dyarchy', and different people have differing opinions as to where the ultimate governing power lies. One town councillor protested that 'we don't even own a spade', and that the County Council holds the power of veto over any major undertaking that the Borough Committee may propose. But another councillor, who is also a riding member on the County body (but is not a local resident) thinks otherwise. He sees the local council, i.e. the Borough Committee, as independent to the extent that it 'controls its own revenue and spends it', despite the fact that the revenue is actually collected and administered by the County.

The truth would seem to lie somewhere between these points of view. Certainly the 'parent' body holds all major items of capital equipment for construction and maintenance, and it employs the key technical experts whose services are necessary in all the County Council's spheres of activity. The County too, under the Counties Act, receives and administers certain monies other than rates. And in all these matters it is bound to its regional (county) responsibilities and cannot properly favour one area over another. On the other hand, precisely because the County Council is responsible for the fair and proper administration of all its constituent ridings it can be called to task if it fails in this.

The machinery of 'riding' representation helps to ensure this, and it is here that Tokoroa has obtained certain (justifiable) advantages over county towns. Apart from provision, under the Empowering Act, for the Tokoroa riding member to be elected triennially by popular vote (instead of election by town committee, as for a County Town), additional representation is permitted and this place falls to the Mayor as Chairman of the Borough Council, or Borough Committee as it should more properly be called. Moreover, the Tokoroa riding assumed yet another advantage just before the 1971 local body elections when it was granted an additional riding member, making 3 in all.[2]

Only one more technicality needs to be mentioned before we focus upon the Borough Committee, its work, and its tribulations. The old Counties practice of 'plural voting', a privilege granted to farmer ratepayers in New Zealand many years ago, still obtains in county elections and therefore still applies to Tokoroa. An 'equity' of 4001 dollars or more gives a person the right to 3 votes; a resident householder with small equity has only 1 vote— a law which is not only unjust but which complicates enrolling procedures. This anomaly, it is said, will be abolished throughout New Zealand in 1975. Meanwhile, in the words of the County

Council Chairman, 'it conflicts with our so-called democracy in which every man is supposed to be equal'.

The Tokoroa County Borough strikes its own rate demands according to estimated costs of maintaining and enlarging the many services and amenities for which it is responsible. Major capital works that require either technical assistance or financial backing from the County Council must, of course, be planned in close consultation with the parent body, a fact which is a sore point with some local councillors. Ordinary property rates account for rather less than half of the Borough's revenus (which stood at about half a million dollars in 1971 and was rising steadily). The balance comes from special rates struck on water, sewerage, and garbage collection services; from central government subsidies (notably the National Roads Board subsidies and more recently, the Petrol Tax), and small amounts from special rates for the use of halls and recreation grounds. Budgetting for the needs of this rapidly growing town is a fairly exacting business. Priorities must ever be balanced against costs, and in the background is 'Big Brother' (the County Council) without whom the Borough Committee would be financially embarrassed and technically limited, and by whom its own hand is somewhat tied.

In presenting the following addresses, given by 2 Borough Councillors, several purposes will be served. An idea will be gained of the scope of work and problems of the Borough Committe. The issue of continuing alliance versus autonomy for Tokoroa will be seen against the background of financial dependence. Certain differences will emerge in the ideology of local political organization. And the familiar problems of political apathy among residents, or the administrators' 'indifference' towards the opinions of the public they are supposed to serve, will be aired.

The first speaker is the deputy mayor and a medical practitioner in the town. The second is the Tokoroa riding representative, a man of considerable local body experience, a Labour Party politician as well, and a farmer. They were addressing the Tokoroa Community Study Workshop in the winter of 1970 and their speeches are recorded verbatim and in full.

THE DEPUTY MAYOR
My object tonight is to tell you what the Council[3] is planning and also to iron out some problems for you. I'm told that Abraham

Lincoln once said, 'You can please some of the people all of the time or all of the people some of the time'. This is no less true of the people of Tokoroa. It has been said that Council shows no interest in your affairs or suggestions. However, I don't feel this is justified—we are interested in all sides of public opinion. The trouble is that so few people step forward and speak; certainly the majority don't, and I think that if they read their newspapers they would find that their criticism is unjustified. Did you know that any member of the public is entitled to go to a Council meeting? You can also attend most of the Committee meetings; you can read the Minutes; you can read the Reports. If you have a specific question or idea, the way to present it to Council is to go and see the administrative officers; you can write a letter, you can ask to appear before a Committee. If members of the public don't like decisions made by Council they can go along and question. There are ways of getting action—much better ways—and these produce a better response than an irate letter written to the editor of a local paper.

There are certain topics I would like to speak on: First, administration: now you will be aware that there is a build-up in assets, personnel and autonomy, meaning independence, and this is scheduled for 1974. This is also the probable date we shall reach 20 000 in population. At this stage we must be self-sufficient in equipment, staff, and experience to run the new city of Tokoroa unaided. Some have said that we should have done these things long ago; I'm not prepared to argue about these things. We have a programme which we can't cut much shorter.

On recreational fields, the Council is taking an imaginative view; some might even call it visionary. We are establishing a Parks Department to substantially upgrade our reserves, to provide glass houses, potting sheds, and housing for our staff; this is in addition to what the Parks and Reserves Department will provide. We will be upgrading our recreational grounds and providing two Rugby League fields, gardens, upgrading the stream, and providing a stand for the sports field. This will cover a large area of land—about 100 acres—and we are also planting a lot of trees. It has been said that this tree planting is a terrible waste—but if you look around you will see we have planted between 1 000 and 3 000 trees over the year and will continue to do this. We are going to establish a tree nursery.

Concerning subdivision, we are upgrading the old sections to the standards of the new ones and this has been a tremendous burden on rates, and we are over half way in our footpath programme and hope it will not take too long to complete. Residents will remember that not so long ago there were no kerbs, only sealing in the very middle of the road; no paths.

Regarding town planning, we freely admit we have made some mistakes and we now feel it is too costly to correct them. We are constantly criticised for them and will no doubt continue to be so. We have done some experimenting; we have experimented with traffic problems and will continue to do so. I have been criticised for being against piecemeal development. We are working in closely with the Ministry of Transport, Traffic Engineers, also Town Planning Engineers.[4] They are going to advise us on the planning for Tokoroa for the future; our playing areas, shopping areas, commercial areas, how much land for this and that.

Cultural: Council has plans to acquire land to build a large Library building. We don't know how we are going to finance it yet. We are assisting the Tokoroa Business Women's Society in their efforts to provide an Art Gallery and will provide a nation-wide art contest, one of the things being that if you make the prize big enough you get a pile of paintings. We are financially assisting 2 bands and we have recently established very reasonable terms for 2 cultural groups for use of halls. Also, as you know, we have arrangements for providing land for kindergartens and play-centres for each primary school and we also own the land the YMCA stands on.

With regard to further publicity and tourism, we are just making a start to this as we have very limited funds. But we hope with the co-operation of the Jaycees and the local businesses involved in this that we can stimulate our tourist industry. There is a lot that people can come here and see, not only in Tokoroa but the sur-roundings. In short, we want Tokoroa to be a good place to visit and live. Recently we have apparently been criticised for letting the location of the Regional Aerodromme slip through our fingers, but I would emphasize that the last shot hasn't been fired in this matter yet and that is one of my concerns; to see that public air services are provided in Tokoroa.

THE COUNCILLOR AND RIDING MEMBER

I would like to speak on planning first. I don't think there is anyone in Tokoroa who could complain of the lack of opportunity to comment on planning. This area, Matamata County, would be the first area which had a disclosed town plan as early as 1961 ... In Wellington today their plan is not disclosed. Every 5 years the plan is reviewed; a public notification is made of the fact that it is reviewed and the details are available at the County Office for anybody who is interested; and it is open for objection. My experience here is that we get a loud and resounding silence and then objections after the period for them is closed. But for those who are interested don't worry! Democracy works locally much better in my view than it does nationally. I won't say anything on the parliamentary field (my ability in that field was unsuccessful anyway) but I have been involved in the local body field for some time. I was involved in the fight for the hospital—now that was a national matter—and everyone of you will appreciate the value that has been to you. Also education—I am a member of an education board. The board may pose suggestions, but the Education Department disposes and that is where the decisions are made. I must say that before 1965 I had no experience of local government whatsoever but since then I have found myself a member of the Tokoroa County Borough, a member of the Matamata County Council, a member of the South Auckland Education Board, and a member of the Tauranga Harbour Board. It is inevitable in that situation that I can take a broad view in this area and I can get my sights outside the boundaries of Tokoroa. It also enables me to utilize and influence with my experience on other bodies. As a member of the education board I am able to assist with the plans for the education of Tokoroa children.

I would like to take issue with the Deputy Mayor if he imagines that Tokoroa will become autonomous, entirely independent by 1974. I would like him to understand that it will be, politically, over my dead body. I think he summarised the programme for development in this town very ably, and from what I have seen and heard of previous discussions I realise that you people know what you want to do, but you will appreciate the tremendous sums of capital involved. As far as I am concerned I will not see capital and ratepayers' good money wasted in chasing after independent status. We have autonomy in this town now; we raise our own revenues and spend it as we like and if anybody thinks you can provide town clerks, engineers, planners, lakes, new parks, rubbish disposal on independence as such, they are wrong! I don't think it is a practicable and politically sound plan by 1974. The Local Government Commission has just been up to Auckland and published its scheme for reorganisation. Four cities have been created, each of not less than 150 000 population (these still have to be granted legislative authority). Nineteen boroughs and 1 city twice the size of Tokoroa have disappeared. It is absolutely essential in my view that local government all over New Zealand should be rationalized. We have had the good fortune here in Tokoroa to set an example which many other boroughs in New Zealand would like to follow. We have had integration of administration and of engineering services, but the local control as a result of county control has been retained. This is what I will always fight for. Local control, local spending, and local raising of rates. I think Council has illustrated the problem very adequately when someone asked what is being done as far as rates are concerned. Rates, of course, are paid to the Matamata County Council and it is responsible for the administration for the whole of this area, including the town of Tokoroa itself. One computer has sent out the rate demands for Tokoroa, the boroughs of Putaruru, Matamata, Morrinsville, Tirau, and the County of Matamata and Piako perhaps as well. Engineering services, equipment—all that sort of thing has to be purchased by a large group of integrated organisations and works and administration integrated. That is my object for this area.

1970 and 1971 were fairly active, even exciting years in Tokoroa local body affairs, and some of the notable events may illustrate not only the preoccupations of councillors but also something of the interpersonal drama of local political life. A little of this is intimated in the second of the speeches quoted above. The councillor and riding member in question is the most outspoken— and possibly the most astute—of the politicians on the local scene. He and the mayor clashed on many occasions over these years: over the Council's community housing project (the Mayor being very skeptical, the councillor firmly believing in the need and principle); over additional riding representation on the County Council (the Mayor at one stage, seemed to take the suggestion as a vote of no confidence in himself); over the acquisition of a new city refuse dump and the whole bungling of public relations that surrounded this and many other matters (see Chapter 8).

The issue of autonomy for Tokoroa was cooled slightly towards the end of 1970, after the County Council had commissioned an independent one-man inquiry into the feasibility of Tokoroa achieving full Borough status. This man, a civil engineer of considerable local body experience, produced his report nearly a year later. He questioned the economic feasibility of autonomy, if the Borough were to sever its important financial and technical relationship with the County. In his report he said:

If Tokoroa is to achieve complete autonomy it must depend on the town's financial ability to stand on its own feet. Costs of establishing Tokoroa as an independent body would be to the detriment of the town at present. The rating potential of the town is not stretched to its limit but in consideration of the paying potential of the young working class population it is getting towards its practical limitation.

South Waikato News, 26 August 1971.

He recommended that Tokoroa should move towards full legal Borough status (to be achieved possibly in 1977) but meanwhile continue to rely on its fruitful alliance with the County Council. Such pivotal questions as town planning would, meanwhile, be in the hands of the County. His report seemed to be anticipating independence without advocating it outright. He suggested a cautious approach, pending the 'new direction' in regional and local body structure which seemed to be emerging from the government sponsored Local Government Commission. The deputy mayor criticised some of the conclusions of the report—especially those which claimed that Tokoroa could not 'pay its own way'. The riding member, on the other hand, supported continuing liaison with the County body and in this he seemed to be supported, at least tacitly, by a majority of the councillors. Even the mayor, whose relationship with both the regular riding member and the County Council as a whole had been somewhat ambivalent from time to time over the past twelve months, seemed to 'see reason' over the big issue of premature independence.

Administrative problems—some of which may also become political issues—are mostly what might be called environmental and utilitarian: the location and cost of a new rubbish dump; traffic control in and around the central service area; the development of a commercial airport; the development of major recreation areas such as the new lake; and 'community housing'—a scheme for the provision of small home units to suit single and retired people and childless couples. The local bi-weekly newspaper gives full and lively reportage of all local political discussion and events, but, as has been suggested, there seems to be little interest and participation among the vast majority of residents on these or any issues.

In the 1969 University Survey of individuals, only 1 person out of 200 was aware that he had voted in the October 1968 local body elections. Only 1 in 10 knew that they had had the opportunity but had not voted, and 9 out of 10 seemed bewildered by the question. 56 per cent could identify the name of a prominent council member from a list of 6 names (35 per cent tried to and failed, 9 per cent admitted their ignorance. Less than one third of the people believed there was enough information being disseminated on local body affairs. A third thought there was not enough. Rather more than a third had no opinion. So much for local interest and participation in town affairs (Pitt and Swain 1970: 38–39).

However the 1971 elections were more encouraging. Postal voting was instituted for the first time and polling was heavier. The press coverage and the part played by interested sections of the community were lively indeed (for example, one of the service groups conducted a series of 'meet the candidate' evenings). Twenty one candidates contested the ten Borough Council seats (eighteen had in 1968). The previous Borough Committee was composed of seven men and three women, two women being Maori, and Labour. The new Council was likewise composed of seven men and three women. But one of the Maori women had not contested the election. Instead, a pakeha woman (and an Independent candidate) had taken her place. Polling ranged from 4 695 for the most popular candidate to a little over 2 000 for the least popular but still successful. The political 'colour' of the candidates was divided, approximately evenly, between Labour and 'Independents'. Independent

candidates included at least several strong National Party supporters—although these did not, as is characteristic in most
local body elections, run openly on a National Party ticket.
The mayor himself (who was re-elected unopposed for his third
term) was widely known to be a 'National' man. Indeed, in
the following year of the General Elections (1972) he ran for the
Taupo constituency (in which Tokoroa is situated), replacing
the sitting National member of parliament—although he lost
the seat to the Labour candidate (also a Tokoroa man).

The successful candidates in descending order of popularity,
in 1971, were as follows:

Mr D. Foote (Independent candidate) had been a sitting mem-
ber. He had lived in Tokoroa for 16 years. A businessman, aged 38.
He was an inaugural member and past president of the Jaycee
Chapter, and a keen cricketer who played for the Tokoroa
Wanderers Club. He had served on several subcommittees of
the 'Council' and was Chairman of the Parks and Reserves
Subcommittee.[5]

Dr Fursdon (Independent) had lived in Tokoroa for 10
years and had served 2 terms on Council. He was a general
medical practitioner, and a member of the Tokoroa Yacht
Club, Clinical Society, and a School Committee. He was also
the most zealous advocate for local autonomy.

Mr J. Hassall (Independent) had lived in Tokoroa since
1926. The oldest Council member, he had retired from employment with N.Z. Forest Products. He was very interested in
schools and in road safety (was Chairman of the Tokoroa Road
Safety Council and a Ward member for the South Auckland
Education Board). He had been active in many other organisations including Red Cross. As a 'Council' sitting member,
he had served on several subcommittees and was chairman
of the Public Relations Committee.

Mr J. Vickerman (Independent) was a sitting member. He
was the Chief Civil Engineer for N.Z. Forest Products, and a
resident of 11 years standing. He was involved with Civil Defence
in Tokoroa. In these elections he was also a candidate for the
Tokoroa riding seat, but not successful.

Mr P. Thomas (Independent). A sitting member, 33 years
of age and a businessman who had lived in the town for 6 years.
He was President of the Jaycee Chapter and the Birthright

Organisation. He was also a keen soccer player representing Tokoroa in the senior team.

Mrs Parkes (Independent) was a sitting member, a resident in Tokoroa for 18 years and married to a transport operator. She was active in the Crippled Childrens Society and Business and Professional Women's Association.

Mrs L. Wellington (Labour) a housewife, Maori, who had lived in Tokoroa for 6 years. She was Chairman of the Anti-litter Committee, Secretary of the Te Rahui Marae Committee and others. She was also serving on several 'Council' subcommittees.

Mrs H. New (independent but a committed Social Credit League supporter and a parliamentary candidate). A High School teacher, 35 years of age and very lively in community affairs. She had lived in Tokoroa for 5 years.

Mr W. Grant (Independent) was another new member. He was 39 years of age and single, a manager in the motor trade, a past president of the Tokoroa Chamber of Commerce, a member of the Rotary Club, and active in Civil Defence. He had lived in Tokoroa for 9 years.

Mr N. Catt (Independent) was also a new member. An administrator in N.Z. Forest Products, he had lived in Tokoroa since 1962. He was Vice-president of the Tokoroa Golf Club, a former secretary and president of the Jaycee Chapter, a former treasurer of a local school committee and was secretary of the Public Library.

The unsuccessful candidates for the Borough Committee were, in descending order of votes polled: a farmer aged about 50, of very long residence in the district (Independent); a well known trade union secretary—an Englishman (Independent); a 46-year-old 'maintenance planner', also an Englishman and active in several local sports and other organisations (Labour); a 58-year-old Cook Island man who had spent about 10 years in Tokoroa—an ex-school teacher he had become a clerk at Kinleith, and was an elder in the local Mormon church (Labour); a 27-year-old Kinleith storeman who had come to Tokoroa as a schoolboy and was active in trade union organisation (Labour); a 48-year-old Cook Island man, an ex-school teacher who had worked at the mill for 19 years—an elder in the local Seventh Day Adventist Church and active in welfare work amongst Cook Island people (Independent); a 42-year-old Western

Samoan man of long residence in New Zealand—and 10 years in Tokoroa—an insurance agent, active in the local Congregational Church and in parent teacher associations (Labour); a 61 year old mechanic who had lived in Tokoroa for 12 years— active in trade union affairs (Labour); a 44-year-old personnel manager—3 years in Tokoroa and active in P.T.A. (Independent); a 52-year-old mechanic who had lived in Tokoroa for 18 years (Labour); a 44-year-old shopkeeper who had lived in Tokoroa for 20 years—a sportsman and a member of the local Retailers Association (Labour).

No very clear pattern emerges which might throw light on the criteria of success in Tokoroa's local body elections. The most likely immediate advantage seems to be that of previous experience on the Borough Committee. It is also worth noting that the majority of successful candidates are professional or 'business' people whereas the majority of the unsuccessful are 'workers' even though many of them had the advantage of longer residence in Tokoroa.

Following this clue it will be noticed that only 1 Labour candidate of the 8 was successful, and that she is a woman (of Maori ancestry), very active in community organisations and also a 'seasoned' councillor. She polled a very comfortable 3 000 votes. Equally well known, however, was the Cook Island man who also ran on a Labour ticket (but was not a sitting member), and who polled only half that number of votes. When one considers the heavy Labour bias of the townspeople in the General Elections, it seems likely that the people tend to vote for known 'personalities' on the local scene—persons in whom they have confidence or whom they 'fancy' regardless of the party political labels. Labour's poor showing was not the result of inadequate preparation and publicity—nor of any general distaste amongst the townspeople of Labour's ideology and 'image'. But there is another consideration... It also seems likely that, first, the business and professional people in Tokoroa (as elsewhere perhaps) would vote in local body elections in greater numbers proportionately than 'the working man', and that they would vote for 'their own kind' rather than for a working man. Second, and complementary to the first, the voting power of these professional and business people—based as it is (under the 'plural voting' system) on equity—is greater in proportion to the man or woman with little property. A combination of these suggestions and facts goes some way towards explaining the class and colour (political and racial) of Tokoroa's local governing body.

One of the '10-point' proposals put forward by the local branch of the Labour Party during the election campaign provides a somewhat ironic commentary on their own failure to break the 'Independents' monopoly on the Borough Committee...

> We will seek the active participation of qualified persons and representatives of community organisations to take the fullest advantage of their knowledge and resources. We reject any suggestion that councillors are all-wise and infallible and recognise that councillors must consider themselves as trustees for the electors.
>
> *South Waikato News*, 2 September 1971.

Clearly, the sitting councillors are not 'all-wise and infallible'. But they would, by and large, seem to meet the positive criteria mentioned in the Labour statement. Especially, they tend to represent the most active, influential and prestigious of the 'community organisations'. We will take a closer look at these community service organisations in the next chapter.

NOTES

1 Matamata County was among the most prosperous in New Zealand — even before the development of Tokoroa on its southern boundary. It covers a very rich dairy farming area. In 1970–71 the County Council was composed of 13 members — 11 single riding representatives and 2 from Tokoroa riding. The presiding office is that of chairman, and the two most important, fully salaried, positions are those of County Clerk and County Engineer. County Council headquarters and meeting rooms are at Tirau township, 20 miles north of Tokoroa.

2 As there were over 3000 electors in the Tokoroa riding in 1971 compared with 440 electors in the next largest riding (Putaruru), and as Tokoroa's rateable capital value was in 1971 $28 000 000 compared with $18 000 000 for the next highest, the granting of one additional riding member, by the parent body, can be seen merely as a reform in the proper direction of fair representation. Some Borough Councillors wanted 5 riding members as Tokoroa's due (the County Council can have up to 18 members, under the Act).

3 The term 'Council' is often used in speech to refer to the Borough Committee. The County Council, in speech, is often called 'the County'.

4 Town planning is a very ambiguous and controversial subject in Tokoroa (see below and also Chapter 8). The County Council has been responsible for major planning—layout of streets and all service networks, etc. The 'Town Plan' is part of a 'District Scheme' maintained by the County Engineer under the Town and Country Planning Act. Full (non-County) Borough status could, presumably allow the Borough Council to execute its own planning.

5 The Borough Committee (often referred to as the Council) handles certain specialised areas of concern by the usual means of subcommittees of its own members. Thus, the Parks and Reserves Subcommittee, Works Subcommittee, Public Relations, Promotion, and Hall and Libraries Subcommittees.

Community Service 8
and Community Action

A closer look at the nature of voluntary participation in community or civic service. The Jaycees etc. The University Survey and 'Workshop'. Needs and possibilities for community action. The role of the newspaper and radio station in community affairs.

Tokoroa Jaycees have launched a 'sponsor a doctor' project in the hope of alleviating the present serious shortage of medical practitioners in the town.

The Chapter has called a meeting for June 25 between leading civic authorities and interested groups to discuss all aspects of the situation. Those invited . . . will be local doctors, representatives of the Waikato Hospital Board, Tokoroa County Borough, N.Z. Forest Products Limited, Chamber of Commerce and the Superintendent of Tokoroa Hospital.

(. . . *News item,* 1970)

Two families lost practically all their possessions when fire gutted a house at Amisfield early last Friday. . . . As the dawn rose over frozen ashes of the razed house. . . Tokoroa's Red Cross swung into action with radio appeals for clothing (and) blankets for the homeless fire victims.

By mid-morning donations of clothing, mattresses and bedding were flooding into a hastily set up depot. Help also came from N.Z. Forest Products housing division which arranged temporary accommodation in house-starved Tokoroa until a permanent home can be found for the families.

(. . . *News item,* 1970)

An ambitious scheme designed to provide the Maori people of Tokoroa with a much-needed amenity is being launched by the Nga Waka Marae Committee. . . it is hoped that following a number of enterprising projects Tokoroa's Maori community will have

a place at which they can meet and entertain visiting friends
from throughout the country.

(. . .*News item*, September 1971)

In a more general way (see Chapter 4) we surveyed the kinds of
community service availabe to the residents through joining the
various clubs and associations which residents themselves have
established and we tried to assess the extent of this participation.
Here, an attempt is made to understand the significance of some of
these activities—their contribution to community development,
and the 'quality of life' in Tokoroa. Considerable emphasis will
fall upon the work of the Jaycee Chapter—not because they are the
only active, community-orientated organisation but because they
are perhaps the most active, and their members are also the most
active in local body politics.

The contribution of specialist service groups such as the St
John Ambulance Brigade, the Volunteer Fire Brigade, and the
Civil Defence Unit, is of great importance to the town but space
forbids much further description here. Their work has been a
response to popularly acknowledged and clearly understood community needs. Both the 'St John' and the Fire Brigade emerged
very early in the history of the community.[1] The former has been
closely associated with the needs of both sport and the industry
(which has one of the highest accident rates of all industries),
and enjoys a subscription membership of about 1000. The Fire
Brigade serves the whole residential area (the company having its
own fire control organization for plant and forest) but its importance must be seen against the special hazards of a town almost
surrounded by easily ignitable forests.

Other specialist groups, most of them very small, but with a
core membership of several dedicated people, can only be mentioned. Most are local branches of wider institutions and they
include such organizations as: the Crippled Children, Intellectually Handicapped Children, and Plunket Societies; the
Prisoner's Aid and Rehabilitation Society (formed at a special
meeting in the local Courthouse in 1971); Alcoholics Anonymous;
the Marriage Guidance Bureau (see Chapter 4); the Family
Budgetting Society (supported by the Lions and the Businessmen's
Association) and the 24-hour emergency Counselling Centre.

Special mention should be made of the local branch of the N.Z.

Red Cross Society which has a thriving Junior section for both boys and girls. Their humanitarian concern is not confined to the local community, but, as is shown by the second news item at the head of this chapter, they are ready to apply themselves locally when the need arises, as of course are many organised groups, even those with only a partial community service function.

A little has already been said (in Chapters 3 and 4) about the Maori organisations, notably the Maori Women's Welfare League and Te Rahui (Nga Waka) Marae Committee. The latter was formed in 1954 and its main objectives have been to help Maori residents with problems of housing, general and child welfare, and education. At least one of its members enjoys the status of honorary welfare officer and social worker, and works in close co-operation with the Department of Maori and Island Affairs. Even the local police have been known to seek advice and to co-operate with leading members of this committee of fifteen or so men and women.

Of the other, the 'civic service' groups, the Jaycees is the longest established in the town and, with the Lions, is acknowledged to be the most active in community welfare. Its two-fold purpose is community service and the fostering of community leadership. The Tokoroa Chapter was established in 1957 and one of its first projects was the construction of an infants' swimming pool. In 1961 the Jaycees organized their first social survey of Tokoroa in order to assess community needs, and on the basis of its findings the Chapter worked away at various projects over the following seven years. It planted trees in public places, developed and equipped at least one public playground, organized Tokoroa's first Arts Festival, helped establish a town brass band, and organized many debates and seminars. By 1969 the Chapter had 'run out of ideas'[2]. Then came 'Operation Information', the comprehensive social survey organized as a joint venture amongst representatives of all service groups, churches, the town council, and the University of Waikato. The Jaycees played a prominent part in promoting the new survey, and have since used the results as a basis for further community activity. Early in 1970 they planned a tour of inspection of all parks, with members of the Borough Committee, to find out what Tokoroa had and needed to have, and to find out where the Jaycees could help with special projects. They also embarked upon a membership drive to increase their numbers, (which then stood at a little over fifty), to a target of seventy. Membership is ostensibly open, requiring only nomination by existing members.

The Jaycees say that they like to have a 'cross section' of keen young men, that is, members from all occupational groups. But in fact, their membership is heavily weighted toward those in business and the professions. Maoris are seldom attracted to such organisations, for fairly obvious reasons (although there has been at least one member in recent years). It is very likely, although difficult to establish, that active membership in the Jaycees (or in Rotaract, Rotary, Lions, or Chamber of Commerce) is a means of becoming fully accepted, socially, in informal networks of businessmen and professionals about town. Certainly membership facilitates such networks and these are almost certainly used by some members, to advance their influence and their status in local body affairs.

In the field of local body politics the Jaycees, like the other service groups, seldom participate directly as an organization, although individual Jaycees and members of other service groups have served on the town council—one as the Mayor in fact. (And the Chamber of Commerce nominated a candidate in the 1971 local body elections.) In the winter of 1970 the president of the Jaycee Chapter was already talking of the desirability of groups such as his becoming more directly involved—at least to the extent of attending, as a body, town council meetings. Since then they have in fact become more active as a service group close to the local political arena.

The Tokoroa branch of the Lions Club was established in the early sixties and eight years later (in 1970) had a membership of between forty and fifty. This group is perhaps not as fully committed to civic service as is the Jaycee Chapter, but is nevertheless often very effective. Their own social gatherings, and their community service, seem to be marked by a greater sense of fun and bonhommie than those of other civic groups. This may be a reflection of the rather older, more mature, and 'relaxed' personalities who are attached to the Lions. Their regular fund raising session, in which the appointed 'Tail Twister' for the evening extorts money from members by way of fines imposed for 'Un-Lion' conduct, is an occasion for considerable mirth, wit, and occasionally embarrassment. Their community projects, directed usually toward fund raising for worthy causes, are often imaginative and tinged with humour or the comic. The most well-known is the Paddy's Market, but the Lions' repetoire is considerable. As the president claimed (in 1970) 'Our morale as a club is high, as is our club image in the eyes of the public'. But, as with the Jaycees, membership is almost entirely European, and business-professional people predominate even though there is no attempt to be exclusive, at least not in Tokoroa.

While the Jaycees and Lions are examples of fairly dynamic service groups, the Chamber of Commerce appears to be the least flourishing of this class and during 1970 it narrowly escaped extinction by 'apathy'. After surviving a crisis in membership (which at its inauguration in 1965 was eighty), and in attendance at its meetings (which were reduced to five), this group rallied with a promise to 'campaign live issues'. Their inventory of such issues is interesting: the problem of a monopoly, by one hotel company, of the liquor licenses in the town; Tokoroa's need for a commercial airport; the provision of more employment opportunities for school leavers, and facilities for higher technical education. The following year (1971) it was still trying to promote live issues and was engaged in devising an alternative plan (to that commissioned by the Borough Committee) for the town business centre.

Much of the diverse flow of energy, community spirit, and good intention found focus for a time in 1969 in 'Operation Information', headed locally by an imaginative and energetic young Roman Catholic priest. The scheme, for putting Tokoroa under the scrutiny of a full scale sociological survey, was hatched by local civic service organisations, churches, and the Borough Committee, in conjunction with the sociology department of the University of Waikato. A very impressive series of exercises followed in November of that year. The town was fully prepared by the local Survey Committee of 'Operation Information' for the invasion of social science students armed with questionnaire schedules. The local radio station, the local newspaper, voluntary organisations of many kinds, the Borough Committee, schools, and many of the householders co-operated magnificently over the several days of the survey. For those caught up in the enthusiasm of this time, Tokoroa was on the verge of truly 'knowing itself', and that knowledge was to be power, power to solve concrete problems, to command the future, and to correct what was be- lieved by many to be the unfortunate and undeserved image of a crude frontier settlement. Tokoroa was in the limelight as a progressive town, admittedly not perfect, but grappling with its 'growing pains' in a positive and 'scientific' manner. For the socio- logists at the University this was a significant step forward in the application of social science to real life human situations, and a 'living laboratory' for them and their students.

The main survey report appeared in due course (and the Youth Opinion survey report a little later), but this was something of an anticlimax. Some local supporters found the format and language of a sociological survey report to be rather formidable stuff, although it does seem that since this initial reaction various local groups have 'done their homework' on their copies of the report and have found some of the information useful. The professor who had overall responsibility for the university's contribution made news worthy points in his general report, and provided material for a front page article in the South Waikato News (15 October, 1970). But the gap between the particular and statistical (of the formal survey report) and the sociological 'overview' was not easy to bridge, and the anticipated 'feedback' of self-knowledge into the community was not forthcoming. The university staff continued survey and other work in the community in 1970 and 1971 (notably the inquiry into Samoan migration and adjustment, financed by the Nuffield Foundation). But rapid increases in student numbers at the university, with a shortage of teaching staff, precluded any further sustained research in the town. Liaison was maintained throughout 1970 and 1971 between local people and a few of the university staff but this lapsed badly after the departure of a key figure from the Tokoroa scene—the Catholic priest.

There was one other possibly significant development which started in the early winter of 1970. At the invitation of the local Survey Committee (see above), the university conducted a series of four 'Community Study Workshops' in the town. Active pro- motion by the two best-known members of the committee—one the young Catholic priest, the other the editor of the town's news- paper—produced a workshop roll of between forty and fifty people of varied ages and status, people who appeared to be sincerely concerned with the welfare of their town. Several Maori and Pacific Island people attended one or more of the sessions, although their numbers were disproportionately low for the town. A minimum of content was supplied by the sociologist conducting the workshop. Discussion groups on the first night examined their own social experience both prior to and subsequent to living in Tokoroa. They were asked to assess their personal social needs in terms of these experiences. Features of 'good' community life, for them, meant:

1 More opportunities to meet people, a variety of people.
2 Freer social exchange between people; fewer barriers; less class distinction.
3 Freedom from the fear of being 'snubbed' or looked down on.
4 More opportunities for self-expression and achievement, for adults and children.
5 Easy access to shopping, entertainment and health services.
6 Freedom from too much pressure to conform (no one likes being obliged to do this or that).
7 Enough privacy if and when one wants and needs it.

Some emphasized the importance of place or environment as helping or hindering good community life. Others stressed that it is people who make good community life. Another important point was the difference in social habits and needs between kinds of people—between old and young, between single and married, between European immigrant and Kiwi, between Maori and Pakeha, and, of course, differences between individuals in any of these groups. Some groups stressed neighbourhood as a special problem area—a 'touchy' area with problems of young mothers, of loneliness, pride, frustration, and a place where friends and enemies are made, and where children may help to break down barriers between adults.

The second session was devoted largely to short addresses by people of various backgrounds and experience in the town. Thus, a shift worker, a Pakeha housewife with very young children, a Maori wife and mother, a Cook Island elder, a voluntary marriage guidance counsellor, and a parson, each presented a vignette of life and problems in Tokoroa. The session explored further the nature of common and recurring problems and the trend of this discussion had political implications. For example:

1 The company was both praised and criticised for its housing

policy. Praised for providing security, incentives and opportunity for workers and residents, it was criticised for lack of variety and suitability in house design and in neighbourhood layout, and lack of local play areas.

2 The town administration was criticized for being out of touch with people's needs, with allowing the town to grow at great speed without carefully considering plans for the community's needs. The council was 'too defensive', 'not progressive enough', and guilty of 'undemocratic' procedures.

3 Residents as a whole were criticised for not speaking out enough on local issues. It was noted that the groups that shout the loudest often shout for the wrong thing—but get their own way.

4 There was an urgent need for more basic services—doctors, preschools, recreation and local shopping services—as the town rapidly 'outgrew itself'.

5 Tokoroa has a 'huge inferiority complex' and receives bad publicity.[3]

The direction which the third session would take had already suggested itself. Seven representatives of powerful or influential organizations in and around the town, were invited to speak on the place of their organization in the life of the community. The deputy mayor represented the town council; a seasoned and well-known local politician represented the County Council; several men and one woman represented civic service groups. There was a top-ranking executive from the company, and also the secretary of the most powerful trade union. Each speaker had been briefed on the direction of the workshop's thinking (and the local newspaper had given the subject fair reportage). Each person's talk was informative in itself but the most interesting and significant development over the course of this session was the emergence of sharp differences in objectives among representatives of several of the most influential groups. Members of the workshop were treated to a spectacle which reminded them, most forcibly, that the powerful 'they' who 'run this town' were by no means in agreement on fundamental issues. At this meeting the first open challenge was issued, by the County man, on the issue of complete autonomy for the borough (see previous chapter). This hit the front page on the next issue of the local newspaper. But there was also the charge, from a prominent citizen, service club leader, and ex-councillor, that 'democracy in this town is non-existent'. And the question of a town plan ('what shape is Tokoroa going to take?') also became a controversial issue at this meeting.

The final session, at which an urban geographer from the university was also invited to speak, concentrated on two major, linked issues. At this session the sociologist for the first time made some specific suggestions. The subject of 'town democracy' as a process, and the town plan as an immediate concrete objective, became the bases for suggested political action by residents themselves. Principles for such action were presented and discussed. The urban geographer described the function and importance of planning for urban growth and the importance of peoples knowledge, discrimination, and choice, in this planning process. The session ended with the Catholic priest taking the initiative by calling a public meeting to discuss, with all parties responsible, the controversial town plan. He also organized a residents' action group to keep this dialogue going.

The action committee was formed and a successful public meeting took place some six weeks later. A lively debate had begun over the shape of Tokoroa's future. Although this particular action group did not survive (possibly due to the departure of the priest at the end of that year), the idea of resident action and of the conscious shaping of a better environment for people was abroad in the town.

Before closing this chapter something must be said about the community function of the local newspaper and the local radio station.

The radio station IZO, operated by the New Zealand Broadcasting Corporation, is the more pervasive of the two media. It is probably listened to (or rather, heard), by a greater number than read the paper.[4] Its programme is heavily weighted towards 'pop' music and local commercial advertising and the announcers are invariably cheerful and 'racy'. In its more conscious community service function the radio broadcasts local news (including Borough Committee affairs), announces most major sporting, cultural, and fund-raising events, helps to promote civic responsibilities in such activities as anti-litter and road safety campaigns, and reminds local electors to enrol (see also examples at the head of this chapter and below). As a 'cool' medium,[5] managed with some sensitivity to the all-round needs of a youthful population, the idea of its contributing something to community welfare and civic consciousness ought not to be overlooked.

The bi-weekly *South Waikato News* is more strenuously and consciously directed towards community and civic service even though it owes its existence largely to income from advertising. The full coverage of sporting and cultural events in the town, which occupies several pages of almost every issue, can be regarded as an important community service. It also encourages people to take the paper. But in addition to these kinds of reporting, the paper provides a very full and prominent coverage of all significant civic and community affairs. It reports on County Council meetings at which Tokoroa Borough matters are discussed, and Borough Committee meetings where, for example, a heated debate may surround the problem of providing low-cost housing for pensioners. It has kept residents as fully informed as it could on all issues and events affecting the town—from expansion programmes and industrial conflict at Kinleith to the administrative complexities and shifting opinions which surrounded the experimental closure of a street in the shopping centre and its conversion into a pedestrian 'mall'. In all this, the editorial policy of the paper appears to be one of impartiality. There are no 'editorials' as such, although on one occasion, the editor was constrained to make a direct statement in defence of his editorial policy. The events surrounding this occasion are instructive, and germane to the theme of this chapter . . .

Early in 1970 the County Council advertised in the local newspaper its intentions to purchase a costly farm property (its exact location not indicated) for use as a refuse dump for Tokoroa, and 'objections' were invited to be lodged by a certain date. It was bound by law to advertise thus; there had been no other communication of the County's intentions, and the Borough Committee (actually the Works Sub-committee) was implicated in what seemed to be a 'conspiracy of silence' and high-handed action on the part of the governing bodies. So the newspaper, taking up arms against the County and the Borough, sought out the necessary facts surrounding the scheme to purchase the farm, and published them in a blistering front-page attack. The mayor was incensed and levelled bitter recrimination against the newspaper. The publicity, he claimed, '. . . was mischievous in its intent and was not in line with good reporting'.

This counter attack was given full front page space in the next issue of the newspaper (26 February, 1970), while on the same page the editor replied under the heading 'Over Sensitive on Public Issue'. His closing remarks are most pertinent...

After a round of heated discussion, charges and counter charges, the public now has most of the facts on the proposal. If any good has come out of it, it may be that the council as a whole may wake up to the fact that it has a lot to do in the field of public relations.

And, on the very same page, there was not only a 'release' of the facts by the 'Council' (Borough Committee) but the following news item as well:

Press to see Behind Borough Scenes
The Tokoroa Borough Council has agreed to a request by the South Waikato News to open Committee[6] meetings to the press. The request by the South Waikato News was endorsed by the Daily Post[7] and Radio IZO.
The request, in the form of three letters from the respective news media, outlined the benefits of opening these committee meetings to the press. These benefits included a more comprehensive coverage of council affairs and a better understanding of council decisions by members of the public...

At the annual conference of the New Zealand Community Newspapers Association in 1972, the *South Waikato News* (now owned by the big Independent Publishing Group), was judged the best all-round community newspaper in New Zealand. This was the sixth time it had won the award in the twelve years of its existence. By examining its role in the context of community affairs one can appreciate the value of such a newspaper in the life of a town, especially a rapidly growing town such as Tokoroa. It takes its place among the agents of community service and community action.

NOTES

1 The St John Ambulance Association was formed in Tokoroa in 1952, although there was a St John first aid group before that time. Active membership (in 1971)

stood at nearly 50 seniors (22 ambulance and 27 nursing) and over 100 cadets (boys and girls).

The Volunteer Fire Brigade was first formed in 1945

2 According to the Jaycee president, addressing the Community Study Workshop in May 1970.

3 The Town Council and service groups had already addressed themselves to this problem. The Jaycees had begun a campaign for 'selling Tokoroa's image' abroad with suitable information. The Council had appointed a Public Relations Officer.

4 The 1969 Survey estimates are not very helpful indicators. The responses for week-night leisure activities' among the adult sample included only 2.4 per cent who listened 'regularly' to the radio, 44 per cent who listened 'occasionally' and 53 per cent who 'never listened'. But, I would suggest that the radio (not necessarily tuned to IZO) is much more popular as a day time 'companion'.

5 A 'cool' medium is one which invites a more complete and active response in the process of perceiving and understanding the message itself. See Marshall Mc-Luhan's *Understanding Media* for the full social significane of this.

6 'Committee' here, refers to sub-committees of the Borough Committee (here referred to as the 'Borough Council'). The Borough Committee meetings are, by statute, always open to the public and the press.

7 The *Daily Post* — a provincial paper with wide circulation, published in the city of Rotorua.

A Reflection on People and Boom Towns[1] 9

(Those) 'who create a town think in terms of numbers and labour force... they tend to forget that the numbers they are dealing with are people'.

> Dr Edmund Leach, addressing the Tokoroa Rotarians,
> August 1970.

Industrial communities in the new world are synthetic communities in the sense that they are created, usually from scattered and culturally disparate human material, to serve the needs of industry. The newer forestry-based communities of New Zealand are fair examples. Unlike the traditional small communities they are not rooted in common kinship, or (to any profound extent) in a common world and life view.

Industrial boom towns have been a feature of New Zealand life for twenty years or more. Men and their families are recruited to them from a wide variety of countries and cultures. The family man seeks to 'better himself' financially and, less often, vocationally. He and his wife face many *social* uncertainties in this search for material security, increased status, and better opportunites for their children—a search which may drive them from town to town and region to region several times in their married prime.

What specifically has drawn people to the timberlands region? Single men and youths have sought high wages and perhaps adventure in a variety of occupations. Young married couples too, have sought a higher income with relatively cheap housing and the chance to save. Young professionals and skilled tradesmen have sought experience and career advancement. The region is a 'seller's market' for the man offering his skills and his labour. For over twenty-five years people have migrated to Tokoroa: New Zealand Maoris from the neighbouring Bay of Plenty and East Coast regions, and from North Auckland; Pakeha New Zealanders from every corner of the country; United Kingdom and Continental migrants; Cook Island Maoris, Canadians, Australians. For some, this has meant a sojurn in the region before moving to more congenial parts of the island. But many remain, and more keep coming.

Just as the industrial organizations compete for markets for their product, so too do they compete for labour and skills. Whatever else might persuade a man to stay one, two, or ten years in a community, serving an industrial organization, one thing is sure—his dependence upon a market system of labour, skill, and product will be one important factor in determining his choice. Professional 'spiralism'—and thus geographical mobility —occurs both within and between organizations, helping to give a fluid character to the populations of industrial communities. More noticeable is the geographical mobility of semi-skilled and unskilled labour. In new industrial communities such workers would seem to contribute most to the youth and 'high masculinity'; the elderly, the middle aged, and women are under represented.

Both the turnover rate and the lopsided age and sex structure provide problems. Persons moving into a new social environment must work at establishing themselves, at being accepted, and at feeling accepted. For some this is hazardous work and a strain upon personality. It may take months or even years for a person to feel secure amongst a network of such hardwon friends. Whether or not the mobile worker and his family are socially skilful and confident, too frequent a change of social milieu must affect the range and depth of the social relationships which they manage to establish.

Likewise the characteristic age structure imposes certain handicaps, although it also carries advantages. Absence of the elderly, the grandparent generation, may mean a denial of access, for young mothers and children especially, to a source of advice and consolation or simply just a change and a refuge from immediate family pressures.

'Although in the conventional pakeha community senior citizens are not accorded any roles of importance by the population at large, they do have potential importance both in the community at large and within the smaller family group. In the community they are a pool of talent for civic, welfare and interest activities

and groups, and in the family they are grandmothers and grand-
fathers, young adults' links with their family past and with the
folklore—however much at variance it may be with the
contemporary ideology of childrearing—and moral support
helpful in childbearing and childrearing, young children's link
with the past. A nearly complete absence of older people may well
be an unfortunate imbalance in any community. (Pitt and Swain
1970: 19).

The accent on youth probably raises the tempo of work and
social life and gives a certain fluidity and flexibility to status
relationships. There could be more striving to 'get on', to 'im-
press', to compete. Youth too places greater demands upon a
range of services—commercial, educational, medical. The problem of an excess of males, especially of that age range so typical of
our forestry camps, needs no elaboration.

In the mushroom growth of an industrial boom town, the 'slow
wisdom' of traditional community life is not possible. The boom
town is a synthetic community. Its inhabitants have not all been
nurtured in its rhythms and its rules. Most have had to *adjust* to
these, and adjust much more rapidly than people have been
accustomed to over most of human history. There are many
merits in the new and expanding social and cultural environment.
There can be stimulating variety and a pattern of status and
prestige which is more fluid than in most traditional communities. A premium may thus be placed upon open-mindedness,
initiative, and talent. But there are also many hazards. The
social casualty rate measured in terms of loneliness and apathy,
whaka maa[2], and frustration, is probably very high—much higher
than in the older communities. A Tokoroa woman, wife of a professional forester who had had six shifts in five years, explains.

... For the older child and the parents, particularly the wife,
the most difficult aspect of frequent shifting lies in the change of
friends. It is sad to make good friends and find that they are
suddenly gone and the whole process must start all over again.
For shy people this must be a very serious burden. It is less
difficult for the husband. He starts off with his work-mates, but
for his wife, unless she is an outgoing person, it can raise considerable distress. This may show as resentment of the family,
the job, the surroundings, the new house and the employer.

An outstanding characteristic of synthetic communities not only in New Zealand but in many parts of the industrial world, is the diverse ethnic, cultural, and class composition of the residents. In our forest-based communities there are not only the main European and Polynesian categories but within each there exist many sub-cultural categories, including linguistic differences. This raises real problems in communication—not so much in the transmission of the bare utilitarian message but communication in the sense of sharing a wide range of experiences and sentiments, receiving personal assurances, understanding social protocol, and exchanging expressions of wit and humour. Socially efficient communication is intricate and is carried on at several levels simultaneously—even at the verbal level there may be two or more streams of meaning. We know how these modes of effective communication vary between individuals *within* a relatively homogeneous cultural group. They vary between social and occupational classes, between male and female, between generations. When peoples from widely differing cultural and linguistic backgrounds suddenly become neighbours it is little wonder that one or other of the parties, or both, will be subject to *whaka maa* when confronting one another in certain social situations. Women seem more vulnerable in this than men. Probably men's work allows them to build up a meaningful system of shared experiences and the language that goes with it.

The need for shared experiences is important. Sport provides one very fruitful area out of which people of otherwise diverse cultural background can and do build bridges of communication and these new industrial communities are noted for their early and rapid development of associational life centred around recreation. Fortunately, this problem begins to resolve itself where, in the mixed ethnic public schools of such communities, a new generation shares a wider range of cultural and social experiences. But for adults of the migrating generation the problem often compels them to retreat socially into a small circle of familiar friends and kinsfolk. Kinship 'encapsulation', that is, the maintenance of tight and relatively exclusive social networks of kinsfolk, is almost certainly a fact of life in these communities, especially amongst Maori and other Polynesian residents. Likewise the ethnic voluntary associations such as the Pacific Island Church, provide social islands to which the members repair periodically and bases out of which they and their children can operate (with no less confidence but with more personality strength) to do necessary business with the less familiar social world around them.

Important in the pattern of social exchange which does develop between ethnic groups as distinct as the Maori (and other Poly-nesian) and the Pakeha, are the individual *mediators*, people whose homes are a venue for mixed ethnic sports committees and various meetings, some quite informal.[3]

Social 'class' differences based on income and occupation (and style of residence where that applies) are not particularly significant in shaping the pattern of social exchange in the smaller industrial settlement. To a certain extent this remains true of company towns like Tokoroa where at least a large cross section of employees (staff and non-staff) occupy similar and adjacent company built houses, either on a rental or an own-as-you-earn basis, and where many non-staff employees earn more than staff men, and where there is a wide range of activities in which men of various occupations and incomes 'rub shoulders' together. However, a large and sophisticated industrial organization—like a pulp and paper mill—recruits professionals, businessmen, and others whose styles of living may be markedly more sophis-ticated, whose incomes may be considerably larger, and whose aspirations may differ radically from those of the majority of semi-skilled and even skilled manual workers. This tendency has become increasingly obvious in Tokoroa. Company execu-tives and their families occupy more expensive homes either in the elevated and more mellow part of the town or occupy expensive 'custom built' homes in select areas including Tokoroa's tiny 'nob hill'. In certain new subdivisions the more well-to-do, sophisticated, or socially aspiring residents, whether private businessmen or company executives, are catered for by real estate agents who stipulate a stiff lower limit on the price of homes which buyers will be permitted to erect on these sites. At the other extreme we have neighbourhoods of the oldest, smallest, and least well-repaired company houses, and these appear to be retaining a disproportionate number of non-Euro-pean families, just as the more expensive sites are taken up almost entirely by Europeans. So, a familiar pattern of 'class' segregation (with ethnic parallels) is emerging—around the edges rather than at the heart, for Tokoroa, like most industrial boom towns, is still essentially egalitarian in spirit.

The siting of new settlements in the region has been according to the practical demands of the industrial organization. The human factor has often been neglected. Access to well established service and cultural centres has often been difficult. Three boom towns: the sawmilling town of Murupara, the pulp and paper town of Kawerau, and the milling and pulp and paper town of Tokoroa have suffered in varying degrees from a failure to attract secondary manufacturing industry. Employment for women and school-leavers is thus confined largely to the major industry (where women are not yet employed in great numbers) or to the few governmental and private service industries.[4]

Another failure is in housing layout and house design. The New Zealand answer to housing people is supplied by engineering and animal husbandry; that is, the provision of cheap, sanitary boxes, arbilitrarily partitioned, and hooked up to essential power, water, and drainage networks. All this is set in a few square yards of the flattest grazing land, and is bordered by a road or 'race' along which the breadwinner may be driven to and from the forest or factory where he labours. Spatial relationships *between* such house units, and between these and other facilities— especially those which cater for the needs of young mothers, children, and old people—are matters which have seldom exercised the minds of our town planners.

The industrial community, at least in its initial stages, may give the resident worker security, but this is at the price of certain basic freedoms. If it is a company or a Forest Service settlement the resident must conform to certain rules which he has no part in formulating. He lives in a company or a state house; there will probably be no alternative. Infringement of the only set of tenancy obligations available to him may mean eviction, the loss of his job, and enforced migration. Or conversely, if he loses his job—even if not dishonourably—he will lose the security of the house and again be forced to migrate. Even if the worker remains in his job and in his house fulfilling all his obligations, it would seem that he is seldom encouraged to exercise his full rights in helping to shape and administer the community. I am not suggesting that our typical resident worker always wishes to exercise these rights. Evidence from one small[5] and one large forest-based community, as well as our common knowledge of so-called 'public apathy' in local body affairs suggests that he is generally content to be on the receiving end of government. By the time the town receives a form of local body charter, the familiar political habits of the residents are likely to be well entrenched. The main industrial organization may not assert itself directly in local political processes but its former image of the 'they who run this place' will be transferred to that local body which, although elected, almost inevitably seems to operate well out of sight and out of mind of the great majority of the residents. They may grumble from time to time but they are generally resigned to their seemingly powerless position as when under direct company or departmental rule.

The phenomenon of political apathy, or rather, political inactivity (for I believe that the term apathy is a misleading one to use in this connection) appears to be so widespread in affluent industrial societies as to be unremarkable. Political activity at any level may be defined as the manipulation of power relationships in the pursuit of public goals. However, the power relationships and the so-called public goals in any modern synthetic community must be seen against a background of much cultural diversity. Significant power relationships will be understood only by a favoured minority and be regarded as manipulable by fewer people still. Furthermore, many of the goals are likely to be sectional—reflecting the interests or ideals of those classes and categories of people who have learned to wield power. Add to this the exaggerated conditions of growth and population turnover in a new industrial town. This demands that people make their major investments of time and energy in establishing and maintaining day-to-day social relationships. We cannot then be surprised at this phenomenon which is too loosely described as political 'apathy'.

In summarizing, I would say that the demands of modern industry, in drawing people hither and thither to life in our new towns and neighbourhoods, place considerable stresses and strains upon mind and personality. There would seem to be a limit to the amount of social uprooting and transplanting a people can stand without their beginning to lose some of the characteristics of happily sociable and socially responsible beings.

Do our new towns and particularly our boom towns, provide optimal conditions for people to interact in the course of daily coming and going—around the house and yard and to the shops, the school, the neighbourhood park? Hardly. People are thrown together, as strangers, in a way which is not conducive to easy, frequent, and satisfying social exchange on the one hand, or sufficient privacy on the other. (And most of us require both by turns.) The new towns spawn a multitude of clubs and other cultural activities. This is good. This too, is 'community'—lines of common interest and activity which cut across neighbourhood and even across class and ethnic distinctions. But 'joining' is not everyone's choice and not all can who might like to. For women especially, neighbourhood may remain an important social field and one which could well exercise the imagination of architects and social planners.

Do our new industrial towns actively encourage the settlement of the grandparent generation—even before the current parent generation settles (or *may* settle) into retirement in the community? Do the architects of our boom towns think beyond providing a box and a yard for the working man and his immediate family? What about the extended family of Polynesian migrants? Can we accept that this is, for the people, often a highly desirable social unit and hence worthy of encouraging in the new town environment? Are we prepared to experiment, boldly, in more satisfying arrangements for living?

Finally, what do our new industrial communities do to promote full resident responsibility and control in community and civic affairs? Is too much done by the expert, the planner, the politician? Local body politics are at present the preserve of a tiny minority. The great majority are, if not all apathetic and indifferent, at least resigned and conditioned to leave it to the zealous and practised few. We are, in this respect, the casualties of mass movement and a rapid agglomeration of people. Problems of social adjustment, the search for security and partial answers to the questions 'Who am I?', and 'What am I?', seem to leave little room for active community concern and the exercise of civic responsibility.

Social and cultural arrangements can and must serve the widest and deepest needs of men, women, and children. If they do not do so, they must be shaped and moulded or dismantled and remodelled if necessary, until they do so. The industrial boom town or any new urban area would seem to be the ideal place to experiment in more satisfying forms of living. Through community action the people themselves might participate more directly in the shaping and administration of their urban environment. Some of this community action might be on a small scale and limited to specific and limited purposes—like the local or neighbourhood organization of family preschool groups. Community action may, however, be also more widely ramifying—and political. This would be a very healthy sign; more people sharing more directly in the development and administration of their town or city.

NOTES

1 The discussion in this final chapter is drawn largely from papers which the present writer prepared in 1971 (for the N.Z. Forester's Conference) and 1972 (for the 7th N.Z. Geography Conference).

2 *whaka maa* see p. 53.

3 See example of such a neighbourhood 'mediator', above, p. 109 in Chapter 6.

4 The 1969 university survey indicated 300–400 married women who were seeking paid work in the town but were unable to obtain it. Since then, a clothing factory has expanded its plant and one or two others have been established. The largest of these was, in 1971, aiming to increase its staff requirements to 130.

5 Kaingaroa Forest Village (Chapple 1970 Vol. 1).

The following photographs show different aspects of life in Tokoroa — a naturalisation ceremony, a traditional Samoan ceremony, schooling, sport and recreation, and a part of the Kinleith mill under construction.

Bibliography

Burch, W.R., 1969, 'The Nature of Community: and a case analysis of failure' in John Forster (ed), *Social Process in New Zealand*, Auckland, Longman Paul.

Campbell, W.J., 1956/57, *Hydrotown*: the social history of an industrial boom town, University of Otago mimeo.

Chapple, D.L., 1970, *Forest and Village*: work, government and community in Kaingaroa, University of Auckland, M.A. thesis in Social Anthropology.

Chapple, D.L., 1973, 'Small Forest Communities' in *Contemporary New Zealand*, K.W. Thompson and A.D. Trlin (eds), Wellington, Hicks Smith and Massey University.

Douglas, E.M.K., 1965, *A Migration Study of Cook Islanders*, Victoria University of Wellington, M.A. thesis.

Forestry Development Conference, 1969, *Manpower*: report of Forestry Working Party, National Development Conference, Wellington.

Forster, John (ed), 1969, *Social Process in New Zealand*, Auckland, Longman Paul.

Forster, John and Peter Ramsay, 1969, 'Migration, education and occupation: the Maori population 1936–66' in J. Forster (ed).

Franklin, S.H., 1969, 'The Age and Sex Structure of North Island Communities', in J. Forster (ed).

Hughes, Everett C, and Helen M. Hughes, 1952, *Where Peoples Meet*: racial and ethnic frontiers, Glencoe Free Prees.

'Hunn Report', 1960, Report of the Secretary of Maori Affairs, Department of of Maori Affairs, Wellington, Government Printer.

Kennedy, D., 1951, 'Forest Practice: Review and Preview', in *N.Z. Journal of Forestry*, Vol. VII, No.3.

Lowry, Ritchie P., 1965, *Who's Running this Town?* Community leadership and social change, 2nd edition, New York, Harper Row.

Metge, J., 1953, The Changing Pattern of Maori Population, *Te Ao Hou*, No.4, Autumn 1953.

Millar, J.P., 1958, *The Towns and Tributary Regions of the Central North Island*, University of New Zealand, M.A. thesis in Geography.

New Zealand Census of Population and Dwellings 1966, Vol. 1, 'Increase and Location of Population', and Vol. 10, *The New Zealand People 1966*, Wellington, Government Printer, 1968 and 1971.

New Zealand Journal of Forestry, Vol. VI, No. 1, 1949.

New Zealand Royal Commission on Forestry 1913, Report, Wellington, Government Printer.

N.Z. Listener, January 20, 1967, 'The Town That Went Boom'.

Pierce, B.F., 1969, *Maoris in Industrial Technology*, University of Auckland, Ph.D. thesis in Social Anthropology.

Pitt, David C., 1970, for Tokoroa Development Committee, 'Operation Information', *An Interim Report on Youth Opinion*, University of Waikato Working Paper in Sociology, No. 5.

Pitt, David C., and Cluny Macpherson, 1971, *Voluntary Separation and Ethnic Participation*: Samoan migrants in urban New Zealand, Nuffield Foundation Ethnic Relations Project, Preliminary Report No. 1.

Pitt, David C., and D.A. Swain, 1970, for Tokoroa Development Committee Operation Information, *An Interim Report to Tokoroa on Community Development*, University of Waikato, Working Paper in Sociology, No. 3.

Report of the Commission of Inquiry into Housing, 1971, Wellington, Government Printer.

Robb, J.H., and Anthony Somerset, 1957, *Report from Masterton*: results of a social survey, Masterton Printing Company.

South Waikato News, Tokoroa Independent Publishers Group.

Tokoroa Jaycees (Inc.), *Tokoroa: Inquire Within 1970–71 and 1972–73*, Tokoroa, Tokoroa Printers Limited.

Whitelaw, J.S., 1961, *A Survey of Kawerau*: its present and future development, for the Tasman Pulp and Paper Company, Kawerau.

Index